ISRAEL, GOD AND AMERICA

by

David Stein

Zion
Publishers

Israel, God and America
Published by Zion Publishers, Inc
Pearland, Texas

Scripture taken from the NEW AMERICAN STANDARD BIBLE(r),
(c) Copyright 1960, 1962, 1963, 1968, 1971, 1972, 1973, 1975, 1977,
1995 by The Lockman Foundation. Used by permission. (www.Lockman.org)

"A School Principal Speaks Out" has been taken from a quote by Principal Jody
McLoud of Kingston, Tennessee (Used by written permission).

ISBN 0-9723596-0-5

Copyright © 2002 by Zion Publishers, Inc

Printed in the United States of America.

ACKNOWLEDGMENTS

To Tom, Sue, Helen, Carol, Bill, John, my wife and my friends from all over the world who have constantly given me encouragement to write this work.

CONTENTS

PART II

To the many who are searching for answers as to what, where and how God is working and moving in the world today; and for those who desire to know in their experience the eternal purpose of God being manifested in and through the lives of His people and His land.

INTRODUCTION

If someone told you the conflict engulfing Israel, the Arab nations, the Palestinians, and the world today was foretold in a prophecy written more than 3,000 years ago would you believe it? Most people would not. Yet, what is taking place today in the Middle East regarding Israel was prophesied in the book of Psalms thousands of years ago.

Behold, Your enemies make an uproar, And those who hate You have exalted themselves. They make shrewd plans against Your people, And conspire together against Your treasured ones. They have said, "Come, and let us wipe them out as a nation, That the name of Israel be remembered no more." For they have conspired together with one mind; Against You they make a covenant." Psalms 83:1-5

What makes this Psalm so remarkable is that from 70 A.D. until 1948 the nation of Israel did not exist. For almost 2,500 years there was no nation of Israel, no national homeland for the Jews, yet incredibly, the Lord caused Asaph, the Psalmist, to write of the coming time in human history when Israel would once again become a nation.

Yet, how can a nation be resurrected that has become extinct and its people removed from its land for thousands of years?

Can an extinct animal suddenly reappear on the earth? Impossible! History is replete with nations that have fallen and been forgotten, never to rise again.

Incredibly though, generation after generation, the Jewish people though dispersed among the nations, maintained their bloodlines, heritage and culture and somehow, miraculously, they survived.

Then suddenly the impossible happened.

On a single day in May of 1948 the nation of Israel was reborn. Through an act of preservation unparalleled in human history, the extinct nation of Israel was resurrected and rose to become a nation among nations. For the first time in almost 2,500 years the Jewish people had a place they could truly call home. Israel, the literal land of

ix

their forefathers, no longer occupied and ruled by foreign powers and abounding with hundreds of years of their own history and heritage, became their homeland and nation once again.

However, the Psalm further prophesies that when the appointed time came for Israel to be resurrected from the ashes of human history, the Arab nations would covenant together with one mind and one purpose saying, "Come, let us wipe them out as a nation, that the name of Israel will be remembered no more."

Here, in this single verse is revealed the heart and soul of the conflict today as the Arab nations, the Palestinians, the European Union, and the United Nations have all conspired together with one mind, for one purpose, "To wipe Israel out as a nation, so the name of Israel will be remembered no more!"

Very few understand the foundational issue between Israel, the Arabs that inhabit parts of Israel, calling themselves Palestinians, and the Arab nations. Because the heart of the conflict is not about peace but a covenant to destroy the nation of Israel, this problem defies human solution.

Recent history has revealed this truth as all the plans, meetings, and proposals for peace in the Middle East by Presidents, Prime Ministers, Foreign Ministers, Secretaries of State, Kings, Princes, the United Nations, the European Union, the Arab Nations, and the United States have had the same outcome – failure.

Why is there seemingly no answer to the conflict raging between Israel, the Arab nations, and the Palestinians? Why does this problem seem to defy human wisdom, human understanding, and human solutions? The reason why there is no solution to these problems is revealed clearly in Psalm 83. The real issue is not about peace, and never has been. The first foundational issue in the conflict is not about exchanging land for peace, and not about the creation of a Palestinian State. It is about the existence of the State of Israel.

The Arab nations seek to wipe Israel out as a nation.

Viewing the daily news through the eyes of man, the conflict that is raging today between the Jews and the Arabs is simply over a small piece of land – Israel. However, the underlying issue in this conflict is a spiritual issue and not a human one. The conflict is a "covenant issue," between Israel, the God of Israel, and the nations.

"I will establish My covenant between Me and you and your descendants after you throughout their generations for an everlasting covenant, to be God to you and to your descendants after you. I will give to you and to your descendants after you, the land of your sojournings, all the land of Canaan, for an everlasting possession; and I will be their God." Genesis 17:7-8

Whose land is it? Who has the right to decide? Is it the United States, the European Union, the United Nations or the Arab nations? Who is the final arbitrator? Will it be the God of Israel, based upon His covenant promises to Israel, or will it be the will of the nations who will decide this issue?

Who will prevail in this conflict, the will of God or the will of man?

The LORD nullifies the counsel of the nations; He frustrates the plans of the peoples. The counsel of the LORD stands forever, The plans of His heart from generation to generation. Blessed is the nation whose God is the LORD, The people whom He has chosen for His own inheritance. Psalm 33:10-12

The conflict raging in Israel and the Middle East today has to do with only one thing – God's plan for Israel in the last days! All the nations are seeking a human solution, which has failed, because their plans are contrary to God's covenant plan for His people, His land, and His holy city, Jerusalem.

Many Americans are beginning to understand that some of the same nations who are seeking the destruction of Israel are also seeking the destruction of America and the free world. The Islamic nations speak of peace, yet they sent forth their Islamic merchants of death to kill thousands of innocent American men, women, and children on September 11th.

Only when events are viewed through the eyes of God from a biblical perspective can a person gain insight and understanding of God's plan for Israel, for America, and for the nations in the last days. Only when you have a true understanding of God's plan for Israel and for America, which is one of the nations, will you be prepared for the horrific events that are about to come upon this world.

God is going to be magnified through Israel to all the nations, and Israel is His war club. The Lord is about to shake the nations for the sake of Israel and His chosen ones.

> *The portion of Jacob, (Israel) is not like these; For the Maker of all is He, And of the tribe of His inheritance; The LORD of hosts is His name. He says, "You are My war-club, My weapon of war; And with you I shatter nations, And with you I destroy kingdoms.*
> *Jeremiah 51:19-23*

Events taking place in Israel and Jerusalem hold the key to the future of all mankind because it is the place where one day, in the not too distant future, a king is going to come to Jerusalem, the promised Messiah.

The Messiah, the Prince of Peace, for whom we yearn, will establish His everlasting kingdom in the city of Jerusalem. It is fitting that His capital will be Jerusalem, a city whose very name means "city of peace."

King Messiah is coming to His chosen people, the seed of Abraham, through whom all the nations of the world will be blessed. The day is fast approaching when the world will know that there is a God in Israel, and that He is returning to His people, to His land and to His holy city Jerusalem, where He will rule and reign forever!

Come! Walk with me, as we explore what God has written about His plan for Israel and America (and the other nations) in the last days.

PART ONE

CHAPTER 1

ISRAEL AND THE LAND

Recorded history tells us that in the year 70 A.D. the nation of Israel like the dinosaur ceased to exist and became extinct. For almost 2,500 years the Jews were displaced and dispersed throughout the nations of the world. Expelled from their homeland and unwelcome in any other, they were without any realistic hope of ever having a nation or homeland of their own again. Why would they? History is replete with nations fallen and forgotten. Incredibly though, generation after generation, the Jewish people maintained their bloodlines, heritage and culture and somehow, miraculously, they survived. And then the impossible happened.

On a single day in May of 1948 the nation of Israel was reborn. Through an act of resurrection unparalleled in human history, the extinct nation of Israel was resurrected to become a nation among nations. For the first time in almost 2,500 years the Jewish people had a place they could truly call home. Israel, the literal land of their forefathers, no longer occupied and ruled by foreign powers and abounding with hundreds of years of their own history and heritage, became their homeland and nation once again.

HOW COULD THE IMPOSSIBLE HAPPEN AFTER ALMOST 2,500 YEARS?

The impossible became possible because the Lord prophesied (i.e. foretold) that it would. Recorded in a book called the Bible, we read that God called forth a prophet by the name of Ezekiel who prophesied that this incredible miracle would take place 2,500 years before it actually did.

At the end of World War II, more than 6 million Jewish men, women, and children, were systematically slaughtered in the Nazi concentration camps. Entire families were murdered and buried by the

1

thousands in mass, unmarked graves. It appeared that the only thing left of the entire European house of Israel was bones.

In approximately 560 B.C. the prophet Ezekiel saw those bones in a vision the Lord gave him. Ezekiel wrote down the vision including the plan the Lord revealed to him regarding those bones some 2,500 years in the future! In 1948, the vision became reality and those bones became the *resurrected nation of Israel* as described in the book of Ezekiel.

> *Then He said to me (Ezekiel), "Son of man, these bones are the whole house of Israel; behold, they say, 'Our bones are dried up, and our hope has perished. We are completely cut off.' "Therefore prophesy, and say to them, 'Thus says the Lord GOD, "Behold, I will open your graves and cause you to come up out of your graves, My people; and I will bring you into the land of Israel. "Then you will know that I am the LORD, when I have opened your graves and caused you to come up out of your graves, My people. "And I will put My Spirit within you, and you will come to life, and I will place you on your own land. Then you will know that I, the LORD, have spoken and done it," declares the LORD.'" Ezekiel 37:11-14*

Just as the prophecy declared, "These bones are the whole house of Israel, dried up, and our hope has perished, and we are completely cut off." The hope of the Jewish people had perished in the ovens of the Nazi concentration camps. "The house of Israel was completely cut off." Yet, the Lord had not forgotten nor abandoned the Jewish people. He said, "*Prophesy to them. 'Thus says the Lord God, "Behold, I will open your graves and cause you to come up out of your graves, My people; and I will bring you into the land of Israel.'"*

The Lord had prophesied that He would bring His people up out of their graves, and that He would bring them into the land of Israel.

Notice, the Lord was very specific about whom it was that He would bring up from their graves. He said He would bring up "His people-the Jews," out from their graves, and He would "bring them into the land of Israel," not Palestine.

Think how incredible the words of this prophecy are today! Notice the Lord said the land of Israel. There was no "land of Israel," from 70 A.D. until May 1948! Yet the Lord declared in His word thousands of years ago that He would bring His people "Into the land of Israel."

Why did the Lord do this? He gives us the very clear answer Himself, *"then you will know that I am the LORD, when I have opened your graves and caused you to come up out of your graves, My people."*

The Lord wanted all of Israel to remember the prophecy of Ezekiel 37:14 about Israel, to understand its meaning and to acknowledge the faithfulness of God. No matter what circumstances or events would transpire, the Lord would never forget nor forsake His everlasting covenant with the Jewish people regarding the land of Israel!

God declared that after almost 2,500 years He was the one who would place His Spirit within His people, and He would place them once again on their own land, the land of Israel.

The Lord spoke it, He had Ezekiel write it, and He declares, "I have done it!"

WHOSE LAND IS IT?

What right does Israel have to the land? The answer to this question is central to the problems that beset Israel, the Palestinians, the Americans, the United Nations, and the entire world.

Presidents, Prime Ministers, kings and the European Union along with the United Nations have all come forth with logical arguments about the rights of the Palestinians and how in order to bring peace to the Middle East, Israel must make hard sacrifices, exchange land for peace and divide Jerusalem.

WILL DIVIDING JERUSALEM AND THE LAND OF ISRAEL BRING PEACE TO THE MIDDLE EAST?

The hatred of Jews by the Arab nations has existed for thousands of years and indeed has only grown deeper and waxed stronger as the centuries have gone by. Will Syria, Egypt, Saudi Arabia, Iraq, Iran, Pakistan, Lebanon, and the other Muslim nations of the Middle East

3

suddenly end their hatred of Israel if a Palestinian state were to be created? Would these nations suddenly change their politics and policies and cease their efforts to destroy the nation of Israel?

The question of Israel's right to the land and Israel's right to exist as a nation are at the very heart of this issue. In light of the situation in the Middle East today, and amid the multitude of voices claiming jurisdiction, who then has the ultimate authority to determine what right Israel, or for that matter any other nation or people has to the land? Who will be the final arbitrator of this issue? Will it be the United Nations? Will it be America? Will it be the European Union? Will it be the Arab Nations?

We maintain the final arbitrator will be the Lord God, Himself!

WHAT IS MEANT BY THE WORDS "THE LAND"?

As we begin our journey to find the true answer to this question, we must define what we mean by the word *"the land."* What *land* are we talking about?

In the Bible, specifically in the book of Genesis, the Lord gives us some of the dimensions of the land to which we are referring.

> *On that day the LORD made a covenant with Abram, saying, "To your descendants I have given this land, from the river of Egypt as far as the great river, the river Euphrates." Genesis 15:18*

On many occasions the Lord referred to this land as *"the land of Canaan."* For those who know geography, they will recognize that the land God promised Israel is considerably larger than the land that the nation of Israel occupies today.

Why has this land been the site of seven wars since 1948? What is it that makes this piece of real estate so important that the Arab nations would seek to conquer it and destroy the nation of Israel five times in 54 years?

The land was barren in 1948 when Israel became a nation. It was a land without any great cities, a land with very few inhabitants, a land with no great rivers, and a dry and hot land almost completely devoid of natural resources.

Yet, the land of Israel is a piece of real estate unlike any other on the face of the earth. It is so important to the Lord God of Israel that He says in His word that He never takes His eyes off of it. His love for the land He gave Israel as an eternal inheritance is revealed in Deuteronomy 11.

> *"But the land into which you are about to cross to possess it, a land of hills and valleys, drinks water from the rain of heaven, a land for which the LORD your God cares; the eyes of the LORD your God are always on it, from the beginning even to the end of the year."*
> *Deuteronomy 11:11-12*

Note in these verses that the Lord said He gave the land to the Jews for one specific purpose, to possess it.

To possess the land means to take control, to occupy, to build cities, to plant vineyards, to rule over it and all the inhabitants of the land, and to use it to the glory of the Lord God of Israel.

All the nations of the 21st century should take note of the fact that the Bible declares that the *"eyes of the Lord God of Israel are always on the land,"* from the beginning of the year to the end of the year.

TO WHOM DOES THE LAND BELONG?

Going back to the very beginning, it is appropriate to ask the question, *"To whom does the land belong?"* The Lord makes the answer abundantly clear.

> *'The land, moreover, shall not be sold permanently, for the land is Mine; for you are but aliens and sojourners with Me' Leviticus 25:23*

5

If indeed *the land* belongs to the Lord, then He is the only one that can rightfully give it away. If you and I own a car, a house, or any other tangible piece of property, it is under our control to decide to whom we will give or sell it. God reserved the same rights for Himself that He gave to you and me!

The very first sentence of the Bible declares that the Lord God created the heavens and the earth. Man did not create anything and is, himself, created by God.

The earth did not evolve out of thin air or the vacuum of space. God created it! And God, as the creator, is the owner of the heavens and the earth and all that is within them. The Lord makes this very clear.

> *PRAISE the LORD! Praise the LORD from the heavens; Praise Him in the heights! Praise Him, all His angels; Praise Him, all His hosts! Praise Him, sun and moon; Praise Him, all stars of light! Praise Him, highest heavens, And the waters that are above the heavens! Let them praise the name of the LORD, For He commanded and they were created. He has also established them forever and ever; He has made a decree which will not pass away. Psalm 148:1-6*

The Lord clearly declares in His word that the land is His creation, His possession and therefore His to do with, as He will. The next logical question to ask then is, "to whom was the land given?" We find the answer in Genesis.

> *And the LORD appeared to Abram and said, "To your descendants I will give this land." So he built an altar there to the LORD who had appeared to him. Genesis 12:7*

GOD'S COVENANT WITH ABRAHAM

God made a covenant with Abraham. But was God's covenant with Abraham a *conditional* covenant, one in which certain restrictions, limits, terms and/or conditions were imposed upon Abraham? The answer is no. When the Lord God of Israel gave the land to Abraham there were no conditions attached to this covenant gift from God. We find that the gift of the land to Abraham and his descendants was *an unconditional covenant with God.* This covenant is described in Genesis 17:7-8.

> *"I will establish My covenant between Me and you and your descendants after you throughout their generations for an <u>everlasting covenant</u>, to be God to you and to your descendants after you. I will give to you and to your descendants after you, the land of your sojournings, all the land of Canaan, for an <u>everlasting possession;</u> and I will be their God." Genesis 17:7-8*

God states twice in these verses that this covenant is everlasting. What does an unconditional covenant mean? It means that the covenant God made with Abraham and his descendants was not based upon the faithfulness of Abraham or his descendents, but based solely upon the faithfulness and promises of the Lord God of Israel!

Yet, there are many today who say that this covenant was conditional. They declare that the covenant was based on Israel's faithfulness to God. The Bible teaches in Psalm 89 that this is not the case.

> *"If his sons forsake My law and do not walk in My judgments, if they violate My statutes And do not keep My commandments, then I will punish their transgression with the rod and their iniquity with stripes. But I will not break off My lovingkindness from him, Nor deal falsely in My faithfulness. My covenant I will not violate, nor will I alter the utterance of My lips. Once I have sworn by My holiness; I will not lie to David. His descendants shall endure forever And his throne as the sun before Me. It shall be established forever like the moon, And the witness in the sky is faithful."*
> *Psalm 89:30-37*

We learn in these verses that God will certainly judge Israel for their disobedience. However, nowhere does it say that because of Israel's disobedience God would violate His covenant with them and that they would forfeit their right by that covenant to the land.

These verses reveal that God's covenant was not based on Israel's faithfulness, but on *God's character, God's promises, and God's word alone! God does not change and He does not lie.*

We find this clearly stated in Malachi 3 and Numbers 23.

> *"For I, the LORD, do not change; therefore you, O sons of Jacob, are not consumed." Malachi 3:6*

> *"God is not a man, that He should lie, Nor a son of man, that He should repent; Has He said, and will He not do it? Or has He spoken, and will He not make it good?" Numbers 23:19*

Anyone who doubts God's faithfulness toward Israel should be reminded of what His word says in Deuteronomy 7.

> *"The LORD did not set His love on you nor choose you because you were more in number than any of the peoples, for you were the fewest and least of all peoples, but because the LORD loved you and kept the oath which He swore to your forefathers, the LORD brought you out by a mighty hand and redeemed you from the house of slavery, from the hand of Pharaoh king of Egypt. Know therefore that the LORD your God, He is God, the faithful God, who keeps His covenant and His lovingkindness to a thousandth generation with those who love Him and keep His commandments; but repays those who hate Him to their faces, to destroy them; He will not delay with him who hates Him, He will repay him to his face." Deuteronomy 7:7-10*

Knowing that the Lord God of Israel is a faithful God, and that He keeps His covenant and His loving kindness to a thousandth generation, is no small promise.

WHICH SON OF ABRAHAM IS HEIR TO THE COVENANT?

Many ask correctly, just who *are* the descendants of Abraham? Scripture records that Abraham had eight sons in all. His firstborn son, Ishmael came through Hagar, his wife's Egyptian maid and his concubine. His second son, Isaac, came through his wife Sarah. Ishmael was the first born of Hagar, and Isaac was the first born of Sarah. From Scripture we learn that the land was not given to the descendants of Ishmael, but rather to the descendants of Isaac!

Abraham loved Ishmael, and when he was seeking the heir to all that was his he went before God saying, *"Oh, that Ishmael might live before you."* However, God's answer to Abraham was very clearly stated in Genesis 17. It was not to be with Ishmael but with Isaac and his descendants, that the Lord would establish His covenant.

> *But God said, "No, but Sarah your wife will bear you a son, and you shall call his name Isaac; and I will establish My covenant with him for an everlasting covenant for his descendants after him." Genesis 17:19*

God had answered and the promises and calling of God are irrevocable. Yet, God did not cast off Ishmael and his descendants.

When Hagar, Sarah's maid, had fled from her presence, the Lord told her she was with child. The Lord described what this child would be like and where he and his descendents would live.

> *The angel of the LORD said to her, (Hagar) further, "Behold, you are with child, And you will bear a son; And you shall call his name Ishmael, Because the LORD has given heed to your affliction. He will be a wild donkey of a man, His hand will be against everyone, And everyone's hand will be against him; And he will live to the east of all his brothers." Genesis 16:11-12*

The Arab nations and their people (the direct descendants of Ishmael), who live to the east of the land of Israel at the dawn of the 21st century are Jordan, Syria, Iraq, Saudi Arabia, Iran, Yemen, Kuwait, and Pakistan. The Lord told us for all time that Ishmael and his descendants would be like a wild donkey of a man, and that everyone's hand would be against them, and they would live east of all their brothers! We learn that the Lord gave a great blessing to the descendants of Ishmael, and indeed today there are more than 12 Arab nations.

"And as for Ishmael, I have heard you; behold, I will bless him, and will make him fruitful and will multiply him exceedingly. He shall become the father of twelve princes, and I will make him a great nation. But My covenant I will establish with Isaac, whom Sarah will bear to you at this season next year." Genesis 17:20-21

Isaac, by God's divine choice was the unique son of Abraham, and to Isaac and only to Isaac and his descendants, would the land of Israel be given as an everlasting possession.

We know that after the death of his wife Sarah, Abraham took another wife. Her name was Keturah. She bore Abraham six sons who are the ancestors of many Arab nations today. God's promise in Genesis 17:4 of Abraham being the "father of a multitude of nations" has most certainly been fulfilled.

Now Abraham gave all that he had to Isaac; but to the sons of his concubines, Abraham gave gifts while he was still living, and sent them away from his son Isaac eastward, to the land of the east. Genesis 25:5-6

We see that Abraham gave all he had to Isaac, but to the sons of his concubines he gave gifts and he *"sent them away from his son Isaac to the land of the east."*

What is the land that is east of Israel? Again, it is the land of Jordan, Iraq, Syria, Iran, Saudi Arabia, Pakistan, Yemen, and Kuwait.

By God's sovereign design and will, Isaac was the *unique son* who became the *chosen one of God* and only his descendants would inherit the land as an everlasting covenant. This promise is repeated to Isaac in Genesis 26:3.

The LORD appeared to him (Isaac) and said, "Do not go down to Egypt; stay in the land of which I shall tell you. Sojourn in this land and I will be with you and bless you, for to you and to your descendants I will give all these lands, and I will establish the oath which I swore to your father Abraham." Genesis 26:2-3

COVENANT PROMISE PASSES TO JACOB NOT ESAU

Isaac married Rebecca and they had twins. The first to come out of her womb was Esau. However, we read in the Bible in Genesis 25:32-34, that Esau sold his birthright as the firstborn son to his twin brother, Jacob for a pot of stew!

The very fact that Esau sold his birthright for a pot of stew showed that he placed little value upon it. As the scripture states in verse 34, *"Thus Esau despised his birthright."*

Later in their lives and near the death of their father Isaac, Jacob received the traditional firstborn's blessing from his father; the blessing which should have gone to Esau, had he not regarded his birthright so lightly and sold it for that infamous pot of stew. Little did Esau realize that when he sold his birthright he also sold and forfeited forever the blessing that went with it.

ESAU'S FAILURE TO HONOR THE GOD OF ISRAEL BROUGHT ETERNAL CONSEQUENCES TO ESAU

"I have loved you," says the LORD. But you say, "How have You loved us?" "Was not Esau Jacob's brother?" declares the LORD. "Yet I have loved Jacob; but I have hated Esau, and I have made his mountains a desolation and appointed his inheritance for the jackals of the wilderness." Though Edom says, "We have been beaten down, but we will return and build up the ruins"; thus says the LORD of hosts, "They may build, but I will tear down; and men will call them the wicked territory, and the people toward whom the LORD is indignant forever." Malachi 1:2-4

The Lord in His sovereignty declared, *"Yet I have loved Jacob; but I have hated Esau."*

To this very day the mountains of Edom in southern Jordan are a completely barren and hostile place. Not only is the land barren but also the Lord says, *"And the people toward whom the Lord is indignant forever."*

The Lord hated Esau because his heart was not right toward the Lord. He clearly had no regard for his birthright as shown in his decision to sell it, nor did he have a heart to serve the Lord. Had Esau loved the Lord and desired to serve Him, he would have treasured his birthright, understood its value and not sold it for a mere pot of stew.

The Arab nations have long argued that the birthright and blessing still belong to the descendants of Esau because Esau was the firstborn. However it is not always the firstborn who is chosen by God as the anointed one to receive the blessing of God.

TWO NATIONS IN ONE WOMB

Isaac prayed to the LORD on behalf of his wife, because she was barren; and the LORD answered him and Rebekah his wife conceived. But the children struggled together within her; and she said, "If it is so, why then am I this way?" So she went to inquire of the LORD. The LORD said to her, "Two nations are in your womb; And two peoples will be separated from your body; And one people shall be stronger than the other; And the older shall serve the younger." Genesis 25:21-23

The Lord declared there were "two nations" in Rebekah's womb, two nations and two sons, Jacob and Esau. Through Jacob's line would come the descendants of the Jewish nation.

In Genesis 26 we read that Esau took two Hittite wives and in Genesis 28 we read that Esau saw that the daughters of Canaan displeased his father Isaac; and he went to Ishmael, and married, besides the wives that he had, Mahalath the daughter of Ishmael.

These two nations were struggling with one another even before their birth, and to this very day continue to struggle with one another. Nothing has changed in 4000 years of history.

The Arab nations have actively sought the destruction of Israel and their half- brothers since the day the nation of Israel was reborn in 1948.

12

The very day Israel became a nation Iraq, Syria, Jordan, Lebanon and Egypt attacked Israel, seeking nothing less than the complete annihilation of the Jewish people and the nation of Israel.

Since then in 1956, 1967, 1973, 1982, and 1991 and during the 2000 Intifada, one or more Arab nations have made war against Israel seeking her destruction.

In September of 2000, Yasser Arafat and the Palestinians rejected peace with Israel and declared war on them, and not surprisingly, again sought the complete destruction of the Jewish people and the nation of Israel.

WHY DID GOD CHOOSE JACOB AND NOT ESAU?

God declared to Rebekah while her sons were still in her womb, "The older shall serve the younger." And the younger was Jacob. Let there be no misunderstanding here. God, through His divine will, sovereignty and purpose, choose Jacob over Esau before either of them was born! God did not choose Jacob because he deserved it. He did not choose Jacob because he was better than Esau. Just as through His divine authority and power, God created the heavens and the earth, man and beast; God, as sole creator and proprietor, has the right to choose who will inherit His blessings and possessions. They are, after all, His to do with as He wills.

CHAPTER 2

JACOB BECOMES ISRAEL

The Bible tells us that Jacob was greatly loved by God. In Genesis 28, the Lord appeared and revealed to Jacob who He was, to whom He would give the land and that through Jacob's descendants, all the families of the earth would be blessed.

> *And behold, the LORD stood above it and said, "I am the LORD, the God of your father Abraham and the God of Isaac; the land on which you lie, I will give it to you and to your descendants. Your descendants will also be like the dust of the earth, and you will spread out to the west and to the east and to the north and to the south; and in you and in your descendants shall all the families of the earth be blessed. Behold, I am with you and will keep you wherever you go, and will bring you back to this land; for I will not leave you until I have done what I have promised you." Genesis 28:13-15*

What the Lord promises will always come to pass. The Lord said He would do it and in May 1948, He did.

The Lord appeared to him a second time for the express purpose of changing his name from Jacob to Israel.

In Hebrew, the name Jacob means "supplanter" and for most of his earlier years the name fitted him perfectly. Jacob was a plotter, a schemer and a deceiver. But as he grew in age he also grew in wisdom and, in later life, Jacob chose to surrender *his* will to the will of God.

The name Israel means "governed by God". Jacob's name had been changed by God just as profoundly as his character had been. He was Jacob the schemer no more, but a man who was willingly governed by God.

When the Lord changed Jacob's name to Israel, He also changed the name of the land from "the land of Canaan" to "the land of Israel".

This event takes place in Genesis 35.

> *Then God appeared to Jacob again when he came from Paddan-aram, and He blessed him. God said to him, "Your name is Jacob; you shall no longer be called Jacob, but Israel shall be your name." Thus He called him Israel. God also said to him, "I am God Almighty; be fruitful and multiply; a nation and a company of nations shall come from you, and kings shall come forth from you. The land which I gave to Abraham and Isaac, I will give it to you, and I will give the land to your descendants after you."*
> *Genesis 35:9-12*

For the first time in Scripture we encounter the word *"Israel."* The Lord changed Jacob's name for all time to Israel. What an incredible event that took place here!

WHEN GOD CHANGES A MAN'S NAME, HE CHANGES HIS CHARACTER FOR A SPECIFIC PUPOSE

In Genesis, we read that the day came when the Lord commanded Jacob to leave the house of his father-in-law, Laban. He was to return to the land of Canaan and face his brother Esau. Jacob knew and feared the anger that burned in Esau's heart against him. Many years before, Jacob, the supplanter, disguised himself as Esau and went before their dying father, Isaac, in order to receive the blessing intended for the firstborn.

After traveling with his family for many days, Jacob arrived at the "ford of Jabbok". As darkness fell, Jacob went off to be alone with God. It was to be a night like no other. When the dawn broke the following day, he would be forever changed by the events of that night. This night he would fear for his life and for the lives of his family, and would meet terror unlike he had ever known, face to face.

Now he arose that same night and took his two wives, and his two maids, and his eleven children, and passed over the ford of the Jabbok. And he took them, and sent them over the stream, and sent over that which he had.
Genesis 32:22-23

In these short verses, we learn that Jacob had come to Jabbok, a tributary of the Jordan River, situated halfway between the Sea of Galilee on the north and the Dead Sea in the south.

Jacob knew that his "zero hour" had arrived. Judgment day was just around the corner. His brother Esau who, for a pot of stew, had sold his birthright to Jacob and then, cursing him, vowed to kill him for receiving the firstborn blessing that came with it was fast approaching, accompanied by four hundred armed men.

Jacob arrived at Jabbok where he would face the greatest crisis of his life. He knew that within twenty-four hours he would either be free of the curse and anger of his brother, or he, along with his wives and children, would be dead.

WRESTLING ALONE WITH GOD

The word "Jabbok" means "to pour out," or "to empty out." Understanding that his very existence was in the balance, that night Jacob went out alone to meet God. Separating himself from the ones he loved most, he set off knowing it was time to "get alone with God".

We live in a day and an hour much like that night. Jacob understood the vital importance of time alone with God. Do we?

Like Jacob on that fateful night, Israel, America, and indeed all the nations of the world have come to their "ford of Jabbok!"

Like Jacob, Israel is facing formidable enemies. War has been declared and once again Israel is forced to fight for her very survival as a nation and as a people.

America came to her "ford of Jabbok" on September 11, 2001. While most of the world watched in horror, Americans awoke to find themselves, like Israel, under attack by an enemy who sought the utter and complete destruction of their nation, their faith, and their way of life.

Like Jacob, we as individuals and as nations come to our own "ford of Jabbok". We are all being brought to the place where there is only one thing we can do, and only One to whom we can turn. And He is the same One that Jacob turned to that night so many years ago, when he went out alone to meet with the God of Israel.

The Lord is going to "empty out" the sin, the self-righteousness and the evil that is in our hearts and from the heart of the nations just as He did with Jacob. God is permitting us as individuals, and as nations, to go through a period in human history where we are going to experience tribulation, violence, wars and pestilence for a specific purpose. It is the time when the Lord God of Israel is going to shake the heavens and the earth, and destroy the kingdoms of the nations!

"Speak to Zerubbabel governor of Judah, saying, 'I am going to shake the heavens and the earth. I will overthrow the thrones of kingdoms and destroy the power of the kingdoms of the nations; and I will overthrow the chariots and their riders, and the horses and their riders will go down, everyone by the sword of another.'"
Haggai 2:21-22

God is shaking the heavens and the nations of the earth by bringing them to their "ford of Jabbok". Their "ford of Jabbok," will force them to decide if they are for or against Israel.

In Genesis 12:3 the Lord clearly and unmistakably declares on what basis He will judge the nations of the earth. Their judgment will be determined by their relationship with Israel. Will they bless Israel or curse Israel?

"And I will bless those who bless you, and the one who curses you I will curse. And in you all the families of the earth will be blessed." Genesis 12:3

17

Nations are made up of people. As the Lord God shakes the nations, He allows difficult circumstances to come into our individual lives and uses them *in* our lives so that, like Jacob, our hearts and characters will be changed to reflect His will and His purposes. God is going to bring each and every one of us to a place where we will understand what it means, "*to wrestle with God.*" And, like the nations, each of us will be forced to decide if we will be among those who will bless or curse Israel.

> *Then Jacob was left alone; and a man wrestled with him until daybreak. Then he said, "Let me go, for the dawn is breaking." But he said, "I will not let you go unless you bless me." So he said to him, "What is your name?" And he said, "Jacob." And he said, "Your name shall no longer be Jacob, but Israel; for you have striven with God and with men and have prevailed." Then Jacob asked him and said, "Please tell me your name." But he said, "Why is it that you ask my name?" And he blessed him there. So Jacob named the place Peniel, for he said, "I have seen God face to face, yet my life has been preserved."*
> *Genesis 32:24, 26-30*

Who was this mysterious man who suddenly appeared in the dark of night and took hold of Jacob, forcing him to wrestle with him for his very life? All alone through the long night hours, Jacob wrestled against this man with no one to help him.

Jacob was alone with God! Jacob was wrestling with the Angel of God! Both Jacob and the Angel knew that this was a "*life and death*" struggle, one that would end only when the rising sun dispelled the darkness of the night.

Jacob was not only wrestling in the outward, or physical realm, but in the inward, or spiritual realm as well. Jacob was not only wrestling with the Angel of God in the flesh, but against that which was not "flesh and blood". He was wrestling against the powers and principalities of the spiritual world that ruled in his heart and today rules in the hearts of evil men throughout the world. Jacob was wrestling against his old nature.

He was wrestling against the lies, the division and the deception within himself. He was wrestling against the anger and resentment that he knew was in his brother's heart toward him.

The time will come when each one of us as individuals will, like Jacob, face God alone. He will bring each of us to our own personal ford of Jabbok, and there we will be required to wrestle with God as our deepest and innermost thoughts, fears and feelings are emptied and poured out before Him.

As the morning dawned, the angel cried out to Jacob saying,

"Let me go, for the dawn is breaking." But he (Jacob) *said, "I will not let you go, unless you bless me." Genesis 32:26*

The Lord has said in His Word that there is a limited amount of time in which He is willing to wrestle with us. The Bible says,

"My Spirit shall not always strive with man." Genesis 6:3

The Angel of the Lord knew that when the night was over He would have to leave the earthly realm and return to His heavenly post. His time of striving with Jacob had a limit. Our God is long suffering and gracious, but He warns us there are limits.

I WILL NOT LET YOU GO UNLESS YOU BLESS ME

When he saw that he had not prevailed against him, he touched the socket of his thigh; so the socket of Jacob's thigh was dislocated while he wrestled with him. Then he said, "Let me go, for the dawn is breaking." Genesis 32:25-26

But Jacob said, "I will not let you go unless you bless me." Jacob knew that this was his golden opportunity to secure the blessings of God. Jacob had no assurance that he would ever get a second chance. With an angry and murderous brother and four hundred of his armed men on the way, Jacob, like the rest of us, had no guarantee of tomorrow. We as individuals and as nations are at that exact point in human history. We will either secure the blessings of God, or we will secure the curses of God! It is now or never!

So he (Angel of God) *said to him, "What is your name?"*
And he said, "Jacob." He said, "Your name shall no longer
be Jacob, but Israel; for you have striven with God and
with men and have prevailed." Then Jacob asked him and
said, "Please tell me your name." But he said, "Why is it
that you ask my name?" And he blessed him there."
Genesis 32:27-29

So Jacob seized the moment and received the blessings of God, and for
all eternity Jacob became known as Israel.

Through this blessing his descendants would inherit the land God had
promised them, and for all eternity the land would become known as
the land of Israel.

JACOB GOES DOWN TO EGYPT

A time of great famine came upon the land where Jacob, (now Israel)
was dwelling with his sons. In Genesis 46, God once again appeared to
Israel in a vision and said these words to him.

God spoke to Israel in visions of the night and said,
"Jacob, Jacob." And he said, "Here I am." He said, "I am
God, the God of your father; do not be afraid to go down to
Egypt, for I will make you a great nation there. I will go
down with you to Egypt, and I will also surely bring you
up again; and Joseph will close your eyes." Genesis 46:2-4

Notice the Lord first told Israel he was "not to be afraid" to go down to
Egypt. Second, God said, "for I will make you a great nation there."

Israel obeyed God and went down to Egypt with his entire family. At
the time, his entire family consisted of only seventy people! Yet, the
Lord said He would make Jacob (Israel) "a great nation". Only the Lord
could make a tiny band of seventy wandering shepherds into a great
nation! Then Israel received the most comforting words of all from the
Lord. *"I will go down to Egypt with you, and I will surely bring you up*
again."

As Jacob, now living in Egypt, approached the time of his death, Joseph along with his two sons went to see him. Then Jacob reminded him of the Lord's promises to him in Genesis 48.

> *Then Jacob said to Joseph, "God Almighty appeared to me at Luz in the land of Canaan and blessed me, and He said to me, 'Behold, I will make you fruitful and numerous, and I will make you a company of peoples, and <u>I will give this land to your descendants after you for an everlasting possession</u>.'" Genesis 48:3-4*

Jacob was telling his son Joseph that his descendants would become fruitful and multiply, and that the Lord, as promised, would give "the land" to his descendants as an "everlasting possession." Everlasting has only one meaning...Everlasting!

Israel (Jacob) knew from the verse in Genesis 46:4 that he would die in Egypt and that his youngest son, Joseph, would be there to "close his eyes." Israel did die in Egypt, and as the Lord promised, Joseph closed his father's eyes and brought his body up from Egypt and buried him in the land God had promised Israel and his descendants.

When it came time for Joseph to die, he too desired that his bones be taken into the land God had promised to his father, the land of Israel. So Joseph called his brothers together as recorded in Genesis 50.

> *Joseph said to his brothers, "I am about to die, but God will surely take care of you and bring you up from this land to the land which He promised on oath to Abraham, to Isaac and to Jacob." Then Joseph made the sons of Israel swear, saying, "God will surely take care of you, and you shall carry my bones up from here."*
> *Genesis 50:24-25*

Jacob, the supplanter became Israel, the man governed by God. And as He promised He would, God blessed him and multiplied him and brought him into the land that would forever bear his name ... the land of Israel.

CHAPTER 3

IN GOD'S SIGHT –BONDAGE IN EGYPT

The story of Joseph is an amazing one. Falsely accused and imprisoned as a young man, by the age of thirty he had risen to a position of great prominence in the cabinet of the Egyptian Pharaoh, second in command only to Pharaoh himself. Joseph served the nation and its Pharaoh well and was greatly honored and esteemed in the land of Egypt.

But a new Pharaoh arose in Egypt who did not know Joseph. Over the years, the Lord had so greatly multiplied the descendants of Israel and Joseph that the new Pharaoh feared them.

Out of fear of their sheer numbers, the new Pharaoh commanded that all Israel be enslaved. For four hundred years, and for a specific plan and purpose, God allowed Israel to serve the Egyptian Pharaohs under cruel and heavy bondage. The Bible tells us that in the midst of their bondage, and at the perfect time, God remembered (i.e. thought upon) His covenant with Israel

> *So God heard their groaning; and God remembered His covenant with Abraham, Isaac, and Jacob. God saw the sons of Israel, and God took notice of them.*
> *Exodus 2:24-25*

God remembered His covenant with Abraham, Isaac, and Jacob. He heard the cry of His people. It is an important and wonderful thing to know that we have a God who sees our situation and hears our prayers when we cry out to Him. It is important to remember that our God is a *covenant keeping God!*

Throughout the Bible we come across the phrase *"In My sight."* It is important to remember that nothing happens on earth that is not *"In God's sight"* –good or bad.

God wants us all to understand that everything we think, say and do and the manner in which we live our lives leads us to one of two places.

Either we find favor "in God's sight" or we find disfavor. God took note of and gave favor to His servant Moses in Exodus 33.

> *The LORD said to Moses, "I will also do this thing of which you have spoken; for you have found favor <u>in My sight</u> and I have known you by name."* Exodus 33:17

Moses found favor in God's sight because His heart was right with God. God is looking for those whose hearts are wholly and completely His!

> *For the eyes of the LORD move to and fro throughout the earth that He may strongly support those whose heart is completely His.* II Chronicles 16:9

"Test yourself!" Ask yourself the single most important question in your entire life! Have you found favor *"in God's sight"?*

Your life is an open book before God. You can no more hide from His sight than Elijah could. Your life is a testimony of who you are in the eyes of men and in the eyes of God. Is your heart completely right with God? Or is there some secret sin that you think you are hiding from God?

God is calling you to repent, to turn from your sins (those things that do not honor Him) and confess them before Him. He longs to forgive you and cleanse you from all unrighteousness, to draw close to you and to lovingly guide and protect you. He will bring you out of your bondage to sin and set you free, just as He brought Israel out from their bondage in Egypt to walk before Him *"as a holy nation."* Make it a priority in your life to find favor in God's sight!

GOD DELIVERS ISRAEL FROM EGYPTIAN BONDAGE

We read how the Lord answered the prayers of the enslaved Israelites.

> *The LORD said, "<u>I have surely seen</u> the affliction of <u>My people</u> who are in Egypt, and have given heed to their cry because of their taskmasters, for I am aware of their sufferings. So I have come down to deliver them from the power of the Egyptians, and to bring them up from that*

23

land to a good and spacious land, to a land flowing with milk and honey, to the place of the Canaanite and the Hittite and the Amorite and the Perizzite and the Hivite and the Jebusite. Now, behold, the cry of the sons of Israel has come to Me; furthermore, I have seen the oppression with which the Egyptians are oppressing them." Exodus 3:7-9

The God of Israel is a God who *sees*, a God who *hears* and a God who *acts* on behalf of His people. He said, *"I have given heed to their cry because of their taskmasters, for I am aware of their sufferings!"* The God of Israel is a God who has a heart for the sufferings of His people!

Are we so different from the Israelites of Moses' time? Don't most of us cry out to God when we are in the midst of trials, testing and times of suffering? Are not the nations of Israel and America suffering today? Their mutual enemy has savagely attacked both nations, and their very existence as nations is threatened.

GOD MAKES A DISTINCTION BETWEEN ISRAEL AND EGYPT

What is it that turned God's heart back to His people after four hundred years of silence? What caused Him to come down and deliver them at that particular moment in history?

The reason the Lord turned back to His people is because they began "crying out to Him" to save them and deliver them from the oppression and the bondage of the Egyptians. Just as with Jacob (the supplanter) who became Israel (governed by God), their pain and suffering had caused a change in their very character. They began to repent and seek the Lord with all their heart, with all their mind, and with all their strength.

Do you desire to be set free from the bondage and oppression of the sin in your life, just as Israel cried out to be set free from the Egyptians?

> *COME, let us return to the LORD. For He has torn us, but He will heal us; He has wounded us, but He will bandage us. "He will revive us after two days; He will raise us up on the third day, That we may live before Him."*
> *Hosea 6:1-2*

24

THE LORD ALWAYS ANSWERS THE PRAYERS OF HIS PEOPLE WHEN THEY REPENT AND TURN BACK TO HIM WITH ALL THEIR HEARTS!

Seek the Lord while He may be found. Return to Him that He may restore you and set you free!

The Lord delivered Israel, indeed. He smote the Egyptians with terrifying plagues and delivered Israel out of Egypt by the power of His mighty outstretched arm.

> *And Moses said, "Thus says the LORD, 'About midnight I am going out into the midst of Egypt, and all the first-born in the land of Egypt shall die, from the first-born of the Pharaoh who sits on his throne, even to the first-born of the slave girl who is behind the millstones; all the first-born of the cattle as well. 'Moreover, there shall be a great cry in all the land of Egypt, such as there has not been before and such as shall never be again. 'But against any of the sons of Israel a dog shall not even bark, whether against man or beast, that you may understand how the LORD makes a distinction between Egypt and Israel.'"*
> *Exodus 11:4-7*

The significant point in these verses is that the Lord made a "distinction between Egypt and Israel."

God is able to "Passover" and make distinctions between the clean and the unclean, the holy and the unholy, the faithful and the unfaithful. He said He would make a distinction between Egypt and Israel, and the Bible declares He did just that.

Thus the memorial of the Jewish Passover for the nation of Israel was established. The Passover was such a significant event in the eyes of the Lord that He commanded all Israel to observe it as an *eternal* memorial and feast to the Lord.

> *'Now this day will be a memorial to you, and you shall celebrate it as a feast to the LORD; throughout your generations you are to celebrate it as a permanent ordinance*

25

Seven days you shall eat unleavened bread, but on the first day you shall remove leaven from your houses; for whoever eats anything leavened from the first day until the seventh day, that person shall be cut off from Israel. On the first day you shall have a holy assembly, and another holy assembly on the seventh day; no work at all shall be done on them, except what must be eaten by every person, that alone may be prepared by you. You shall also observe the Feast of Unleavened Bread, for on this very day I brought your hosts out of the land of Egypt; therefore you shall observe this day throughout your generations as a permanent ordinance.'
Exodus 12:14-17

The Lord God of Israel made this a permanent ordinance for all generations to the Jewish people and to the world for some very specific reasons.

The God of Israel is a covenant keeping God who is able to fulfill His promise to bring His people into the land of Israel.

The God of Israel is a covenant keeping God who is able to deliver His people from the hand of all those who seek to oppress, enslave, and destroy Israel.

The hand of God stayed Israel from moving against the Palestinians for eighteen months, despite their daily and unrelenting suicide attacks on innocent Israeli men, women, and children.

However, the ultimate abomination against the God of Israel by the Islamic merchants of death took place on Passover eve, March 28, 2002 in Netanya, Israel: A Palestinian suicide bomber walked into a hotel filled with Jews observing and celebrating their Passover Seder. He made his way into the room by disguising himself, and then detonated a bomb in the midst of the crowed room of people. In the attack, twenty-two people were killed and 140 injured – twenty of them seriously. Hamas claimed responsibility for the attack.

Within a few days, Israel moved against the Palestinian Authority with ferocity that no one expected. Why? Because they had not only attacked Israel, they had attacked the Lord God of Israel and His Holy Passover.

There is a line over which the Lord God will not allow the enemies of Israel to cross. Everything changed in Israel after the Passover massacre. God changed the hearts of the Israeli's from patience to passion and from temperance to action. The enemy had violated the Lord's Passover, and had massacred His people as they honored Him and celebrated His sacred memorial feast. It was a night when the world was once again reminded that the Lord God of Israel is God.

CHAPTER 4

GOD'S PURPOSE FOR ISRAEL

In Exodus 19 God's purpose for Israel was declared to Moses and by Moses to the Israelites.

> *Moses went up to God, and the LORD called to him from the mountain, saying, "Thus you shall say to the house of Jacob and tell the sons of Israel: You yourselves have seen what I did to the Egyptians, and how I bore you on eagles' wings, and brought you to Myself. Now then, if you will indeed obey My voice and keep My covenant, then you shall be My own possession among all the peoples, for all the earth is Mine; and you shall be to Me a kingdom of priests and a holy nation.' These are the words that you shall speak to the sons of Israel." Exodus 19:3-6*

The God of the universe brought His people out of Egypt to be *"His own possession among all the peoples of the earth."* What an awesome thing to be chosen by God out of all the peoples of the earth to be His own possession.

The God of Israel is holy, and those who serve Him must also be holy.

Therefore, He brought His people out of the land of Egypt for a specific purpose. It was God's purpose to bring His people into *"His holy land of Israel so they could become a kingdom of priests and a holy nation."*

The Lord declared in these verses, *"all the earth belongs to Him"* and out of all the peoples of the earth He chose Israel to be His *"own personal possession."*

What an incredible promise to a nation and to a people who had been slaves in Egypt for 400 years. Yet, what God says He will do, He does!

God is a personal and loving God. When He chooses a person or a people, He does it because He wants intimacy with them.

Oh, what a lesson there is for all of us in these verses. God seeks an intimate, personal relationship with His people and that relationship is based on His love for us! Has anyone ever told you plainly, *"God loves you"?* He does! And because He is a God who does not change, that love will never change.

> *"Know therefore that the LORD your God, He is God, the faithful God, who keeps His covenant and His lovingkindness to a thousandth generation with those who love Him and keep His commandments; but repays those who hate Him to their faces, to destroy them; He will not delay with him who hates Him, He will repay him to his face. Deuteronomy 7:9-10*

GOD TESTS ISRAEL

The Lord tested Israel in Judges 3 to see if they would obey His Commandments.

> *They* (the 5 nations) *were for testing Israel, to find out if they would obey the commandments of the LORD, which He had commanded their fathers through Moses. The sons of Israel lived among the Canaanites, the Hittites, the Amorites, the Perizzites, the Hivites, and the Jebusites; and they took their daughters for themselves as wives, and gave their own daughters to their sons, and* <u>*served their gods*</u>*. The sons of Israel did what was evil* <u>*in the sight of the LORD,*</u> *and* <u>*forgot the LORD their God and served the Baals and the Asheroth. Judges 3:4-7*</u>

Israel forgot the Lord their God. In His sight, they began to serve and worship other gods. The consequences for Israel were disastrous! The Lord allowed Israel to be sold into slavery for eight years as punishment for their disobedience.

> *Then the anger of the LORD was kindled against Israel, so that He sold them into the hands of Cushan-rishathaim king of Mesopotamia; and the sons of Israel served Cushan-rishathaim eight years. Judges 3:8*

Disobedience, which is sin, always has consequences for any person or nation who forgets The Lord and serves foreign Gods!

God's covenant regarding the land as an everlasting possession was unconditional. However, Israel's right to live in the land *was* conditional. The condition has been and always will be hearing God's voice and obeying His commandments.

Abraham was greatly blessed by God for one specific reason, which is recorded in Genesis, Chapter 22.

> *"In your seed all the nations of the earth shall be blessed,*
> *because you have obeyed My voice." Genesis 22:18*

This promise to Abraham of blessing all the nations of the earth through his seed was passed down to Israel. And they were told to do two specific things.

#1 - Obey his voice, and
#2 - Keep His commandments

Tragically, Israel did not always obey God's voice nor did they always keep His commandments. The book of Judges all too plainly chronicles their many failures. There is an order to the blessings of God. Obedience to God always precedes His blessings.

Just as God called Israel to be a "kingdom of priests," He also calls each one of us as individuals to that same high calling. I have met many people who clearly knew God was speaking to them, calling them to Himself. I have watched them struggle with God's right to lay claim to their lives, and then sadly watched as they turned away, choosing disobedience over obedience to God.

THE FEAR OF GOD

When men and nations lose their fear (i.e. reverence) of God, they very quickly lose their fear of sin. When we lose the fear of sin, we find ourselves in a very dangerous place ... rebelling against God, against His covenant and against His commandments.

Time and time again the leaders of Israel lost their fear of God. And, in each and every case, this caused them to lead the people of Israel down that perilous road to losing their fear of sin.

ISRAEL WORSHIPS OTHER GODS

The loss of the fear of God led Israel into profound sin, the worst of which was their worship of other gods

Throughout Israel's history, the consequences of disobedience to God's commandments meant removal from the land or slavery and bondage to ungodly kings and nations who occupied it.

God's plan for Israel has always been an eternal plan that will end in their redemption and reconciliation with Him. Israel is suffering the consequences of their sins today because they have lost their fear of God. They have not obeyed His voice nor have they kept His commandments. The Israel of today fears the nations, and has sought the solutions to their problems by seeking the wisdom of man, not the wisdom of God.

Just as in their past, and painstakingly recorded in the Bible, the solutions to Israel's problems today will only be reconciled when they turn back to the Lord their God! Only through repentance and obedience will Israel be delivered from the hands of their enemies.

The Bible and the word of God are living proof to this fact! For thus says the LORD through the prophet Isaiah,

> "As the lion or the young lion growls over his prey, Against which a band of shepherds is called out, And he will not be terrified at their voice nor disturbed at their noise, So will the LORD of hosts come down to wage war on Mount Zion and on its hill." Like flying birds so the LORD of hosts will protect Jerusalem. He will protect and deliver it; He will pass over and rescue it. Return to Him from whom you have deeply defected, O sons of Israel. Isaiah 31:4-6

CHAPTER 5

THE JUDGMENT OF GOD AND THE MERCIES OF GOD

We see that God judged Israel when they were disobedient. However, when Israel repented, He was attentive to their cry. God is always looking for the repentant heart, and most clearly, the repentant heart of a leader who will turn the hearts of His people back to their God. In Solomon's prayer of dedication he cries out unto God:

> *If they take thought in the land where they have been taken captive, and repent and make supplication to You in the land of those who have taken them captive, saying, 'We have sinned and have committed iniquity, we have acted wickedly'; If they return to You with all their heart and with all their soul in the land of their enemies who have taken them captive, and pray to You toward their land which You have given to their fathers, the city which You have chosen, and the house which I have built for Your name; then hear their prayer and their supplication in heaven Your dwelling place, and maintain their cause, and forgive Your people who have sinned against You and all their transgressions which they have transgressed against You, and make them objects of compassion before those who have taken them captive, that they may have compassion on them (for they are Your people and Your inheritance which You have brought forth from Egypt, from the midst of the iron furnace), that Your eyes may be open to the supplication of Your servant and to the supplication of Your people Israel, to listen to them whenever they call to You. "For You have separated them from all the peoples of the earth as Your inheritance, as You spoke through Moses Your servant, when You brought our fathers forth from Egypt, O Lord GOD."*
> *I Kings 8:47-53*

THE ONLY WAY BACK TO GOD IS THROUGH REPENTANCE

These verses contain God's promises to Israel thousands of years ago. They are as valid today as they were then. These biblical verses contain principles about the character of God that has never nor will ever change toward His covenant people.

The Lord does not change, and His plan for Israel has not changed since the day He brought them out of Egypt.

Nothing surprises God. He knew from the very beginning that the Israelites were a stiff-necked people, a proud people who would often forget their fear of God and turn away from Him. So the Lord provided a way back to Him, and the way back to God always begins with repentance.

Solomon's cry unto God instructed Israel exactly what to do in these verses, saying to them, *"Repent! Admit* (confess) *your sins before Me! Admit you have acted wickedly and turn from your wicked ways!"*

Return unto God with all your heart, and with all your soul, and He will forgive all your transgressions and sins! He will maintain your cause O Israel! He will protect you, He will cleanse you, He will set you free and defeat your enemies, and He will restore you because He is your God!

Are we really any different than the Israelites? Has God changed? No! He is calling each of us to do individually what He called the nation of Israel to do.

God is calling each of us *"to return to Him"* and *"to be holy because He is holy."* Holy means that you have a heart for God and are obedient to His commandments.

If you are living in sin the Lord is calling you to do precisely what He instructed Israel to do. *"Repent! Admit your sins before Me! Admit you have acted wickedly and turn from your wicked ways!"*

Just as God commanded Israel, He is commanding you and me to return to Him with all our heart and soul, and He will forgive our transgressions and sins!

33

THE FEAR OF GOD

Abraham was a wonderful example of a man who had the "fear of God."

The word *fear* is used often times in the Bible to denote *reverence*, or a "*reverential awe*." Abraham *reverenced* God. He *honored* God and he *honored* His commandments. Abraham feared God. The book of Genesis, Chapter 22, reveals that the Lord was looking for a man who feared Him, and God made it clear He had found such a man when the angel of the Lord said to Abraham:

> *"Now I know that you fear God." Genesis 22:12*

The Lord told Israel exactly what was required of them in Deuteronomy 10. Now, this may come as a surprise to some of you. You might have thought that God would say; *"Now I know that you* love *Me"* or *"that you* trust *Me."* Over and over again, in both the Old Testament and the New, God declares he wants us to first *"Fear Him."*

> *"Now, Israel, what does the LORD your God require from you, but to fear the LORD your God, to walk in all His ways and love Him, and to serve the LORD your God with all your heart and with all your soul, and to keep the LORD'S commandments and His statutes which I am commanding you today for your good?"*
> *Deuteronomy 10:12-13*

Psalm 111:10 says it all. For Israel, for America, for you and for me - as individuals and as nations, in decisions we have to make as we seek solutions to the problems we face - to fear God is the only wise thing to do.

> *"The fear of the LORD is the beginning of wisdom."*
> *Psalm 111:10*

THE LORD IS A CONSUMING FIRE

God commanded Israel to conquer the land He had promised to them. He told Moses that Joshua would lead Israel into the land and take possession of their inheritance.

'Go up to the top of Pisgah and lift up your eyes to the west and north and south and east, and see it with your eyes, for you shall not cross over this Jordan. But charge Joshua and encourage him and strengthen him, for he shall go across at the head of this people, and <u>he will give them as an inheritance the land which you will see</u>.'
Deuteronomy 3:27-28

Joshua became God's chosen instrument in leading the people of Israel to take possession of their inheritance – the land of Israel. However, to possess the land, they had to conquer it and drive out from before them the nations that inhabited the land. It is important to note that it was not because of Israel's righteousness that God chose them to drive out these nations dwelling in the land God loved. The Lord tells us His reason. It was because of the "*wickedness* of these nations".

"Know therefore today, that it is the LORD your God who is crossing over before you as a <u>consuming fire</u>. He will destroy them and He will subdue them before you, so that you may drive them out and destroy them quickly, just as the LORD has spoken to you. Do not say in your heart when the LORD your God has driven them out before you, 'Because of my righteousness the LORD has brought me in to possess this land,' but it is because of the <u>wickedness of these nations</u> that the LORD is dispossessing them before you. It is not for your righteousness or for the uprightness of your heart that you are going to possess their land, but it is because of the <u>wickedness of these nations</u> that the LORD your God is driving them out before you, <u>in order to confirm the oath which the LORD swore to your fathers, to Abraham, Isaac and Jacob</u>." Deuteronomy 9:3-5

Notice, it was God who declared *He* would destroy the nations and *He* would subdue them before Israel!

Why did the Lord say this? The Lord went before Israel because He knew the nations in the land were stronger, more numerous and better prepared for warfare than the Israelites. Remember, these were men, women and children who had only known the labor of Egyptian slavery. They were servants and brick-makers. They were not educated or trained to do battle with mighty armies.

But the word of God says *"It is the Lord your God who is crossing over before you as a consuming fire."*

Anyone who doubts that God has and will judge the actions of nations should tremble when reading these verses!

The Lord declared that He was going to *destroy* and *dispossess* these nations because of their wickedness before Him!

God is able to dispossess any nation at any time. It is of great significance to note that even when the Lord went before Israel, they still had to cross the Jordan, engage, fight, and defeat the enemy. God would give them victory, but they were not to be idle bystanders. Israel had to *"go forth in faith"* and *"fight the battles in the name of the Lord!"*

MUDDLED BY FEAR OR MOVED BY FAITH

A generation earlier God had commanded Israel *"to cross the Jordan"* and *"possess the land."* God brought the Israelites to a place of decision soon after He delivered them from Egypt.

The Israelites had beheld the miraculous parting of the waters of the Red Sea. They were living witnesses of how they had all walked through the midst of the Red Sea on dry ground. And not only had none of them perished, but they watched Pharaoh's entire army drown before their very eyes. Yet, when commanded to go forth and take the land they'd been promised by the same miracle-working God, they refused to cross the Jordan and engage the enemy.

Why? How could this *be?* It was because their fear of the enemy was greater than their faith in the God of Israel.

THE PROMISES OF THE LORD OR THE REPORT OF MAN

Before God allowed Israel to possess the land that He had promised them, He tested them.

Many people have a hard time with the notion of God testing them. We fully accept this concept in school as a valuable pre-requisite to advancement to a higher grade. Even on our jobs, we take tests to evaluate our skill and proficiency in order to be promoted and move up the company ladder. Why then do we recoil and have such difficulty in accepting that God has tests for us too? Such was the test for the twelve spies of Israel.

The Lord commanded Moses to send out 12 spies, one from each of the 12 tribes of Israel, into the land before them so they could ascertain the strength of the enemy. Why?

Without a doubt, God knew the *exact* strength of the enemy they were to face. God wanted these spies to see for themselves what obstacles lay ahead and how they would report what they saw to the people. It was a test that would reveal much about their faith. God had Moses send out the twelve spies to test their hearts.

The Lord was testing their hearts to see if they believed God and had the faith to go forward, fight the battles in the name of the Lord God of Israel and take possession of their inheritance - the land of Canaan (Israel)!

The Lord was also testing His people. Would they believe the report of man (the spies), and be fearful or would they believe the promises of God and move forward by faith?

> *Then the LORD spoke to Moses saying, "Send out for yourself men so that they may spy out the land of Canaan, which I am going to give to the sons of Israel; you shall send a man from each of their fathers' tribes, every one a leader among them." So Moses sent them from the wilderness of Paran at the command of the LORD, all of them men who were heads of the sons of Israel. Numbers 13:1-3*

The spies reported that there were giants in the land.

> *Thus they told him, and said, "We went in to the land where you sent us; and it certainly does flow with milk and honey, and this is its fruit. Nevertheless, <u>the people who live in the land are strong</u>, and <u>the cities are fortified and very large</u>; and moreover, <u>we saw the descendants of Anak there.</u> Amalek is living in the land of the Negev and*

*the Hittites and the Jebusites and the Amorites are living
in the hill country, and the Canaanites are living by the
sea and by the side of the Jordan. But the men who had
gone up with him said, "We are not able to go up against
the people, for they are too strong for us." So they gave
out to the sons of Israel a bad report of the land which
they had spied out, saying, "The land through which we
have gone, in spying it out, is a land that devours its
inhabitants; and all the people whom we saw in it are
men of great size. There also we saw the Nephilim (the
sons of Anak are part of the Nephilim); and we became
like grasshoppers in our own sight, and so we were in
their sight." Numbers 13:27-29, 31-33*

What kind of report did the twelve spies give to the Israelites upon
their return? Ten of the twelve gave a negative and frightening report.
They cried out saying, "We are not able to go up and prevail against
these people. They are too strong for us! The men of the land are
giants! They are of such great size that we became like grasshoppers in
our own sight as well as in theirs!"

But what about the other two spies, Joshua and Caleb? What was *their*
report?

*Then Caleb quieted the people before Moses and said, "We
should by all means go up and take possession of it, for we
will surely overcome it." Numbers 13:30*

Did these other two spies, Joshua and Caleb, go to the same *places* as
the other ten? Had they seen the same *things*? The answer is a
resounding "Yes"! The crucial difference between these two and the
other ten was that Joshua and Caleb believed the Lord. They
understood that in God's sight, these giants were nothing. Remember,
in Deuteronomy 9, He had told them ahead of time what He would do;
destroy them, subdue them and drive them out.

In this one short verse, one of the most basic and fundamental biblical
principles and truths is proclaimed.

God tests us to see where our hearts are. True faith is not only believing that God's word and promises are true, but it is also *acting* upon them. Simply put, true faith manifests itself as obedience to God.

The Lord was testing the hearts of the leaders of the twelve tribes of Israel. He was testing two specific areas of their hearts, their faith and their obedience to Him!

We are no different from the Israelites! We must all make choices. And every choice we make carries with it two main issues, the issues of *faith* and *obedience*. They are inseparable.

JUDGMENT

Oh, how the human heart recoils at that word! But reasonably and rationally, as with any test, you expect a judgment to be based how you did, right? You either pass or you fail.

Do you think that God is less reasonable and rational than *we* are? The judgments of God are certain and specific, and they have a beginning and an end.

Many people believe and teach that God's promise to Israel (i.e. their inheriting the land) was based upon Israel's faithfulness in obeying His laws. The Bible itself gives clear testimony to the fact that when the Jewish people were disobedient, the Lord judged them, punished them and even exiled them *from* the land. But again, just as His judgments were certain and specific, there was a time frame in which they were operational. God's judgments on Israel had a beginning and an end.

The Bible is filled with testimony from God Himself, that He *never* forgot *nor* rejected His covenant with Israel.

> *'Yet in spite of this, when they are in the land of their enemies, I will not reject them, nor will I so abhor them as to destroy them, breaking My covenant with them; for I am the LORD their God. But I will remember for them the covenant with their ancestors, whom I brought out of the land of Egypt in the sight of the nations, that I might be their God. I am the LORD.' Leviticus 26:44-45*

God's covenant with Abraham was unconditional. Remember, it was God who made the covenant with Abraham, not Abraham who made a covenant with God! God cannot lie, nor does He change His mind.

> *"For I, the LORD, do not change; therefore you, O sons of Jacob, are not consumed." Malachi 3:6*

GOD'S COMMANDS ARE PRECISE AND HAVE ETERNAL PURPOSES

The commandments and statutes, the character and the nature of God never change. God sees sin as sin, whether it's a nation, a people or an individual. There are no exceptions.

In the book of Leviticus the Lord commanded Israel to give the land a *"Sabbath rest every seventh year."* The Israelites were to sow (plant) and reap (pick) the fruit of the vine for six years, but in the seventh year the land was to be given a full year of rest without any sowing or reaping to be done. It was to be the land's Sabbath rest unto the Lord.

> *'Six years you shall sow your field, and six years you shall prune your vineyard and gather its crop, but during the seventh year the land shall have a Sabbath rest, a Sabbath to the Lord; you shall not sow your field nor prune your vineyard.' Leviticus 25:3-4*

The Lord knew that the Israelites would wonder, as anyone would, *what* were they going to eat during that seventh year? So, in the book of Leviticus, the Lord answered, revealing His plan and His promise.

> *But if you say, "What are we going to eat on the seventh year if we do not sow or gather in our crops?" Then I will so order My blessings for you in the <u>sixth</u> year that it will bring forth the crop for <u>three</u> years. When you are sowing the eighth year, you can still eat old things from the crop, eating the old until the ninth year when its crop comes in. Leviticus 25:20-22*

The Lord promised that in the sixth year, He would bring forth a crop that was so bountiful it would be *equal to three years of crops in one year!* What a promise. What a blessing. What a vacation plan. And

40

this is just one example of the promises and the provision of God for *all* those who will obey His commandments and follow Him.

Following God always involves faith, obedience and incredible blessings! Make no mistake about it. The life of faith, obedience, and blessing is a matter of deliberate and daily choices. The Lord makes this abundantly clear in Deuteronomy 30.

> *"See, I have set before you today life and prosperity, and death and adversity, in that I command you today to love the Lord your God, to walk in His ways and to keep His commandments and His statues and His judgments, that you may live and multiply, and that the Lord your God may bless you in the land where you are entering to possess it." Deuteronomy 30:15-16*

The Lord gave Israel a choice, just as He has given you and me a choice. We must all choose either obedience to His Commandments, or disobedience. There is no middle ground with God.

Israel had prospered in the land God had given them. But in their prosperity, they had become proud, powerful, arrogant and self-righteous. The Lord had set before Israel life and prosperity, death and adversity. Why? So that Israel, through *faith* and *obedience*, could live and multiply, and so the Lord could abundantly bless them in the land He had given them. God longs to bless His people but He cannot bless us when we choose the sin of disobedience.

Israel chose to disobey God. They chose to not give the land its year of Sabbath rest. Israel became a nation that decided to "do what was right in their own eyes"; however, what Israel really became was an "abomination in the eyes of God!"

The Lord waited patiently for four hundred ninety years for Israel to turn back to Him. He sent numerous prophets to them, calling upon them to turn back (repent), obey Him and *"to give the land its Sabbath year of rest unto the Lord!"* However, at the end of this period of waiting and calling out to them, the Lord said, "Enough!" God's judgment for their disobedience was at hand.

The books of Daniel and Jeremiah tell us that around the year 586 B.C. the Lord sent Nebuchadnezzar, the ungodly king of Babylon, to destroy Jerusalem and Judah and take them captive. Israel remained in captivity in Babylon for exactly seventy years.

Israel's disobedience was judged, and the price they paid was severe. Removed from the land and taken into captivity, Israel was now *forced* to honor God's commandment and allow the land to receive its Sabbath rest.

This brings us to the interesting question as to why the Lord chose *exactly* seventy years for Israel's captivity in Babylon.

If we divide 490 (years of disobedience) by 7 (every 7th year was to be a Sabbath rest for the land), we come up with *exactly* 70 (years).

There were seventy Sabbath years of disobedience, and there would be seventy years of captivity for Israel. One year of captivity for every Sabbath year of disobedience.

God's judgments are certain and specific, and they have a beginning and an end!

God executed judgment against Israel for one reason. *'Because you have not obeyed My word!'*

> *"Therefore, thus says the Lord of hosts, 'Because you have not obeyed My words, behold I will send and take all the families of the north, declares the Lord, and I will send to Nebuchadnezzar king of Babylon, My servant, and will bring them against the land, and against its inhabitants, and against all these nations round about; and I will utterly destroy them, and make them a horror, and a hissing, and an everlasting desolation.'"*
> *Jeremiah 25:8-9*

God prophesied (i.e. foretold) through the prophet Jeremiah, that He was going to send a ruthless and ungodly foreign king to dispossess Israel from the land. And He did!

THE LORD NEVER KEEPS HIS PLANS FOR HIS PEOPLE A SECRET

God never keeps His plans for Israel and for His people a secret. He reveals them through His word and through His prophets. God revealed as His plan for Israel's captivity, as well as for their return to the land in the amazing prophecy found in Jeremiah, Chapter 29.

> *"For thus says the Lord, 'When seventy years have been completed for Babylon, I will visit you and fulfill My good word to you, to bring you back to this place. For I know the plans I have for you,' declares the Lord, 'plans for welfare and not for calamity to give you a future and a hope. Then you will call upon Me, and I will listen to you. And you will seek Me and find Me, when you search for me with all your heart.'" Jeremiah, 29:10-13*

GOD'S PURPOSE IS TO BRING HIS PEOPLE BACK INTO A PERSONAL RELATIONSHIP WITH HIM!

The chastisement of Israel, by the Lord, had a single purpose, to bring His people back into an intimate and personal relationship with Him. His chastisement was for their welfare, not for their calamity.

Difficult times have a way of opening what would otherwise be, blind eyes, deaf ears and hard hearts. God's judgment sent Israel into captivity for their sin, but His purpose was to cause them to *call upon Him* and to *search for Him with all their hearts* so that intimate and personal relationship between a loving God and His people could be restored.

Do you have a personal relationship with the Lord?
Would you like to?
Call upon the name of the Lord... He will listen to you!
Seek Him with all your heart... you will find Him!

CHAPTER 6

LIFE CHOICES

It is impossible to understand the unfolding of God's purposes for Israel, for America and for us, without seeing our lives through the eyes and heart of God. We need God's perspective, and that can only come from knowing and understanding God's word as written in Scripture.

You must believe by faith that what unfolds for your life began in eternity in the mind and heart of God. This truth can give every moment of your life meaning and an eternal purpose.

Believing by faith that God knew you and chose you before the foundation of the world will give you a true sense of purpose for your life. If you can reach up and take hold of God's promises, you can know with absolute certainty that God is at work in us and around us to bring His promises to pass.

The Lord God confirmed this in His Word through Isaiah the prophet.

> *"Surely, just as I have intended so it has happened, and just as I have planned so it will stand, For the LORD of hosts has planned, and who can frustrate it? And as for His stretched-out hand, who can turn it back?"*
> *Isaiah 14:24, 27*

When God speaks to you there is absolutely no doubt in your mind who is speaking to you. There is no doubt in your mind what He is saying to you or what He is calling you to do.

Doubt is never the issue. The issue is always obedience.

THE CRISIS OF BELIEF

The Israelites, while under slavery in Egypt, cried out to God for deliverance. So God chose a deliverer. One who would stand before Pharaoh and plead for the release of His people. This deliverer's name was Moses.

When the Lord put this call on the life of Moses, it brought him immediately to a point that could best be described as *"a crisis of belief."*

> *Then Moses said to the LORD, "Please, Lord, I have never been eloquent, neither recently nor in time past, nor since You have spoken to Your servant; for I am slow of speech and slow of tongue." Exodus 4:10*

In other words, Moses was saying to the Lord, "Don't send *me* to stand before Pharaoh! I stutter! Send my brother! Send my cousin! Send *anyone* else Lord, just *don't send me!*"

Fear gripped Moses. Excuses and escapes were all he could think of! But the Lord would not allow Moses to deny His calling.

> *Then the anger of the LORD burned against Moses, and He said, "Is there not your brother Aaron the Levite? I know that he speaks fluently. And moreover, behold, he is coming out to meet you; when he sees you, he will be glad in his heart. You are to speak to him and put the words in his mouth; and I, even I, will be with your mouth and his mouth, and I will teach you what you are to do. Moreover, he shall speak for you to the people; and he will be as a mouth for you and you will be as God to him." Exodus 4:14-16*

Notice in these verses that the Lord knew that Aaron spoke fluently, and the Lord put it into Aaron's heart to be filled with joy when he met Moses.

Then the Lord spoke the most important words Moses ever heard. *"I will be with your mouth ... I will teach you what you are to do!"*

God was going to equip Moses and put into his mind and on his lips *exactly* what to say to Pharaoh. All Moses had to do was what he was told to do. In a word, obey. And obedience is of the utmost importance to God.

Moses was instructed to go and stand before Pharaoh in Egypt and repeat God's instructions to him:

"Thus says the Lord God of Israel, *'Let my people go!'*"

I can assure you that when God calls you, you'll know it's the Lord. And you will have only two choices – whether you will be obedient to His call or disobedient. God is always faithful to those who hear His voice and choose to obey Him.

When you hear God speaking to your heart, choose obedience! Reach up and take hold of His promises with all your heart, all your mind and all your strength. You will *never* be sorry you did!

CONFLICTS AND HARD CHOICES DO NOT MAKE CHARACTER

The heart and character of Moses, Joshua and Caleb are not only revealed in what they say, but in what they do. We see one common thread in the characters of all these men. When it came to choosing God's way or man's way, they all chose God's way. Faith and obedience were never an issue.

When conflict and hard choices came, it revealed the character of these men. The truth is conflict and hard choices do not make character. Conflict and hard choices *reveal* the character already in a man's heart! The actions of a man define what he believes. Either you believe God, and act on your belief, or you don't. You either exercise your faith, or you don't!

When the Israelites rebelled against God, Joshua and Caleb spoke out to the people on behalf of the Lord. Their belief and faith in God was revealed as they proclaimed: *"The Lord is with us, do not fear them!"*

> *Joshua the son of Nun and Caleb the son of Jephunneh, of those who had spied out the land, tore their clothes; and they spoke to all the congregation of the sons of Israel, saying, "The land which we passed through to spy out is an exceedingly good land. If the LORD is pleased with us, then He will bring us into this land and give it to us—a land which flows with milk and honey. Only do not rebel against the LORD; and do not fear the people of the land, for they will be our prey. Their protection has been removed from them, and the LORD is with us; do not fear them." Numbers 14:6-9.*

46

Joshua and Caleb pleaded with their people *not* to rebel against the Lord. Joshua and Caleb encouraged them *not* to fear the people of the land because *"Their protection had been removed from them, and the LORD is with us!"*

THE LORD JUDGES DISOBEDIENCE AND REBELLION

After the Israelites heard the bad report about the land from the ten spies, any faith they had was quickly replaced by fear. The people, in their disobedience and rebellion towards God, turned on their deliverer, Moses. They began conspiring to kill Moses, Joshua and Caleb, to appoint another leader over them and, of all things, to return to slavery in Egypt! God reveals to Moses His judgment against the people for their rebellion.

> *The LORD said to Moses, "How long will this people spurn Me? And how long will they not believe in Me, despite all the signs which I have performed in their midst? I will smite them with pestilence and dispossess them, and I will make you into a nation greater and mightier than they." Numbers 14:11-12*

The Lord is testing the heart of Moses. What is the condition of Moses' heart toward this stiff-necked people? How will he respond?

He declares to Moses, *"I will smite them with pestilence and dispossess them, and I will make you into a nation greater and mightier than they."*

Now, if you were Moses, how would *you* have responded? Would you have pleaded with God on behalf of a people who were seeking to stone you to death? Would you have cried out to God to forgive a people who were seeking to find another leader who would lead them back to the very bondage from which they had cried out to be delivered?

During times of persecution and rejection do you seek the counsel of men or of God? It is not what you *say* in times such as this, but it is what you *do* that reveals your character.

MOSES STANDS IN THE GAP

And Moses said unto the Lord,

> *"Now if You slay this people as one man, then the nations who have heard of Your fame will say, Because the LORD could not bring this people into the land which He promised them by oath, therefore He slaughtered them in the wilderness.' But now, I pray, let the power of the Lord be great, just as You have declared, The LORD is slow to anger and abundant in lovingkindness, forgiving iniquity and transgression; but He will by no means clear the guilty, visiting the iniquity of the fathers on the children to the third and the fourth generations.' Pardon, I pray, the iniquity of this people according to the greatness of Your lovingkindness, just as You also have forgiven this people, from Egypt even until now." Numbers 14:15-19*

Moses became an "intercessor" for His people in his act of praying for them. Moses understood the sins of his people, and yet he chose to bear them before God as a loving mediator between sinful man and a holy God. Moses was *"standing in the gap,"* for his people even though they had sinned!

ARE YOU ONE WHO IS STANDING IN THE GAP?

Are you "standing in the gap" for anyone? Are you pleading with God on their behalf?

Are you standing in the gap for your husband, for your wife, for your children? Are you standing in the gap for your nation? Are you standing in the gap for your Pastor or Rabbi? Are you, as God commanded in Psalm 122:6 standing in the gap for Jerusalem? If not, why not?

These are dark days where deception and sin have overcome many and they have lost their fear of God and have fallen into sin.

A generation has arisen in Israel that does not know God. Many do not believe He exists.

48

Ask yourself some important questions? Do you live in a nation where there is little knowledge of God? Do you live in a nation that has lost its fear of the Lord? Do you live in a nation that has lost its fear of sin?

Please ask yourself; do you live in a nation where most people believe that God will not judge them and their nation even though they have grievously sinned against Him?

God is calling each and every one of us to become like Moses, to prayerfully intercede and "stand in the gap" before Him for our families, for our leaders, for our nation and for Israel.

The Lord looks for those, like Moses, who will stand in the gap before Him. He declared this in His word to Ezekiel.

> *"I searched for a man among them who would build up the wall and stand in the gap before Me for the land, so that I would not destroy it; but I found no one."*
> *Ezekiel 22:30*

There is a fundamental biblical principle involved here that we should all understand.

Even though Moses pleaded with the Lord to pardon the iniquity (i.e. sin) of his people, he understood very well that even if the Lord *did* pardon the iniquity of his people, He would not necessarily remove the consequences of their sin.

THE CONSEQUENCES OF SIN!

Our Lord is a merciful God, a loving God, a forgiving God and a restoring God. However, He is also a God who does not remove the consequences of our sins.

> *So the LORD said, "I have pardoned them according to your word; But indeed, as I live, all the earth will be filled with the glory of the LORD. Surely all the men who have seen My glory and My signs which I performed in Egypt and in the wilderness, yet have put Me to the test these ten times and have not listened to My voice, shall by no*

means see the land which I swore to their fathers, nor
shall any of those who spurned Me see it."
Numbers 14:20-23

We see in these verses, the mercy of the Lord when He says to Moses, "*I have pardoned them according to your word."*

God heard Moses prayer, and He answered him according to his words on behalf of the Israelites. Yet, the Lord did not take away the consequences of their sins.

Observe in these verses that the Lord noted and referred to, *"All the men who have seen My glory and My signs which I performed in Egypt and in the wilderness!"* God held the Israelites *accountable* for their unbelief after they personally witnessed the glory of God go before them and the miracles He performed on their behalf!

The Lord declared, *"Ten times they have put Me to the test, yet they have not listened to My voice!"*

Remember, God said He blessed Abraham for one reason, "You have *obeyed* My voice!" The importance of obeying God's voice and trusting Him are the keys to walking with the Lord.

The consequences of Israel's sin for *not* obeying God's voice are revealed in the sentence that says they, *"shall by no means see the land which I swore to your fathers, nor shall any of those who spurned Me see it."*

Think of it! The entire generation of Israelites who rebelled against God would never enter, or even see the land, flowing with milk and honey, promised to them by God's covenant with their forefathers Abraham, Isaac, and Jacob! What a price to pay!

Because of their disobedience, they would never possess their inheritance! As stated before, God's judgments are certain and precise and they have a beginning and an end.

A GOD WHO HEARS

'As I live,' says the LORD, 'just as you have spoken in My hearing, so I will surely do to you; your corpses will fall in this wilderness, even all your numbered men, according to your complete number from twenty years old and upward, who have grumbled against Me. Surely you shall not come into the land in which I swore to settle you, except Caleb the son of Jephunneh and Joshua the son of Nun. Your children, however, whom you said would become a prey— I will bring them in, and they will know the land which you have rejected. But as for you, your corpses will fall in this wilderness. Your sons shall be shepherds for forty years in the wilderness, and they will suffer for your unfaithfulness, until your corpses lie in the wilderness. According to the number of days, which you spied out the land, forty days, for every day you shall bear your guilt a year, even forty years, and you will know My opposition. I, the LORD, have spoken, surely this I will do to all this evil congregation who are gathered together against Me. In this wilderness they shall be destroyed, and there they will die.'" Numbers 14:28-35

Few verses in the Bible tell more about the Spirit and character of God than these.

Notice that the Lord *heard* what the Israelites said against Him. We serve a *"God who hears"* what we say, and He takes note of it.

These verses reveal that God's punishment for all those who grumbled against Him, from twenty years old and upward, would never enter the land of Israel. What was the fate of those who grumbled against the Lord? God said that their *"corpses would fall in this wilderness."* However, God's punishment of them would not affect their children. Their children would be the ones to inherit the land because they were innocent of grumbling against the Lord.

Grumbling against God cost them their inheritance. The Bible reveals to us that when the Israelites were in the desert they complained (i.e. grumbled) *constantly!* One of the things against the Lord that they complained about was that they didn't have meat to eat. The Lord heard their grumblings. Only two men from that generation, Joshua and Caleb, the two spies who *believed* and *trusted* God would live to enter the land and possess their inheritance.

> *Moses said, "This will happen when the LORD gives you meat to eat in the evening, and bread to the full in the morning; for the LORD hears your grumblings which you grumble against Him. And what are we? Your grumblings are not against us but against the LORD." Then Moses said to Aaron, "Say to all the congregation of the sons of Israel, 'Come near before the LORD, for He has heard your grumblings." Exodus 16:8-9*

Instead of grumbling, the Israelites should have built an altar to the Lord and worshiped Him. Instead of grumbling, they should have praised Him for delivering them from slavery and cruel bondage in Egypt; for providing ample food, water, shelter and provision in the journey to their promised land!

What do you do when things do not go right in your life? Do you grumble against God? Do you curse God or do you bless, praise and thank Him? Do you even believe there *is* a God?

To all those who grumble against God, or do not believe God exists, take note of what He says regarding this in Isaiah 45.

> *"Declare and set forth your case; Indeed, let them consult together. Who has announced this from of old? Who has long since declared it? Is it not I, the LORD? And there is no other God besides Me, A righteous God and a Savior; There is none except Me. Turn to Me, and be saved, all the ends of the earth; For I am God, and there is no other. I have sworn by Myself, The word has gone forth from My mouth in righteousness And will not turn back, That to Me every knee will bow, every tongue will swear allegiance." Isaiah 45:21-23*

The nations and peoples of the earth should know and understand there *is* a God. There is no other God besides Him and one day, to Him and Him alone, every knee will bow, and every tongue will swear allegiance.

CHAPTER 7

A MAN WITH A DIFFERENT SPIRIT

"But My servant Caleb, because he has had a different spirit and has followed Me fully, I will bring into the land which he entered, and his descendants shall take possession of it." Numbers 14:24

In this one verse in the Bible we learn a great deal about the character and faith of this man, Caleb. The Lord declares Caleb had a *"different spirit."*

What was so different about Caleb's spirit? The Lord reveals the answer saying, *"Caleb has followed me fully."*

Caleb believed the report of the Lord and stood before the entire congregation of Israel and declared his belief saying,

> .... *"We should by all means go up and take possession of it, for we will surely overcome it." Numbers 13:30*

Ask yourself, are you a man or a woman with a *"different spirit?"* How would the Lord describe you?

Would He say you are a man or woman who has a *"different spirit?"*

The difference between the holy and the unholy before the Lord is having this *"different spirit."*

Abraham, like Moses, Caleb, and Joshua was a man with a *"different spirit!"*

> *And the Lord took him outside and said, "Now look toward the heavens, and count the stars, if you are able to count them." And He said to him, "So shall your descendants be." Then he believed in the LORD; and He reckoned it to him as righteousness. Genesis 15:5-6*

These verses reveal that Abraham *believed* the Lord and it was counted to him as *righteousness*. Abraham's trust in God was so strong that he believed every word that was spoken to him, and he proved it by acting upon it. Abraham, Moses, Caleb, and Joshua were all men who possessed a *"different spirit."*

Men and women of God have always had a *"different spirit."* And what set them apart from the others was that when they heard God's voice, they obeyed.

Do you know the voice of God when He is speaking to you? If you do not know His voice, then you are in trouble at the heart of your relationship with Him.

The entire Bible is filled with verses revealing the fact that *"the Lord speaks to His people."*

Hearing the voice of the Lord is usually *not* hearing the audible voice of God. We hear the voice of God through His Scriptures, through prayer, through worship, through life experiences and through those He appoints as prophets, those whose calling it is to proclaim His message.

All Israel heard God's voice through Moses, Caleb, and Joshua, but many chose not to obey. Choosing whether or not to obey God's voice once you've heard it determines the path and ultimate destiny of your life.

The Lord said everyone must choose whom he or she will serve. Joshua declared it thousands of years ago, and it is as true today as it was then.

As Joshua said to all the congregation of Israel:

> *"Now if you are unwilling to serve the LORD, choose this day whom you will serve, whether the gods your ancestors served in the region beyond the River or the gods of the Amorites in whose land you are living; but as for me and my household, we will serve the LORD." Joshua 24:15*

Whom will you choose to serve?

I can speak from personal experience that when the Lord brought me to my "ford of Jabbok," I had to choose whom I would serve.

God spoke to me, just as He spoke to Moses, Joshua, Daniel and many other men in the Bible. I had the same choice to make as these men did, either to be obedient and follow God, or to turn away in disobedience.

What God called me to do was to quit my job, leave our adult children and grandchildren, our friends, our home and all our worldly possessions and move to a foreign land to do His work among His people.

We are not independently wealthy so we were called upon to walk by faith, relying totally upon the Lord to provide for all our material and financial needs. I *immediately* had a *"crisis of belief,"* just like Moses.

I knew I was no Moses or Joshua, and I certainly was not a Daniel. Yet, by His divine mercy, which is beyond all my human understanding, the Lord called me to go forth.

> *"Son of man, I have appointed you a watchman to the house of Israel; whenever you hear a word from My mouth, warn them from Me." Ezekiel 3:17*

Just like Jacob, when God brought me to my "ford of Jabbok," I was forced to "wrestle with God." I wrestled with my fears, with my unbelief, with my own excuses before the Lord. Just like Jacob, I "wrestled with God," and God won.

It was only after being forced to "wrestle with God," that like Jacob, Caleb, and Joshua I received His blessing and became a man with a *"different spirit."* It was not until I had received a *"different spirit,"* and chose to follow God and obey His commandments that I truly began to experience God.

Israel, from the time of its expulsion from the land and its dispersion throughout the nations of the earth, has been "wrestling with God." For more than 2,500 years, Israel has wrestled with the denial of its disobedience *to* God, its anger *against* God, its unbelief and lack of faith *in* God and its love *for* and relationship *with* God.

> *Thus you will know that I am the LORD; for you have not walked in My statutes nor have you executed My ordinances, but have acted according to the ordinances of the nations around you. Ezekiel 11:12*

The Israel of today is a secular nation, seeking to be like the nations around her. She will never succeed.

This will never be, because it is not God's purpose for Israel to be like all the other nations. God's purpose for Israel is that she be a holy nation, a nation of priests *in* whom and *from* whom all the nations of the earth will be blessed.

Today, Israel is suffering once again because of its disobedience to God. Today, Israel is wrestling with God.

Are *you* wrestling with God? God calls men and nations to wrestle with Him so that they can come to know Him. He is seeking to have a personal relationship with you. He said so in His word.

> *O taste and see that the LORD is good; How blessed is the man who takes refuge in Him! Psalm 34:8*

These are not idle words. God is seeking those whose hearts are wholly His.

> *For the eyes of the LORD move to and fro throughout the earth that He may strongly support those whose heart is completely His. II Chronicles 16:9*

If you want to know God and hear His voice, you must get right with Him!

A HEART FOR GOD

We find a wonderful example of this biblical principle in the book of 1 Samuel. The time had come for the Lord to choose a king for Israel.

What do you think is the one characteristic that the Lord looked for in the man who would rule over His people? It's the one characteristic that the Lord looks for in any man. And that is the condition of that man's heart toward God. In I Samuel 13 we are told that *"the Lord sought out for Himself a man after His own heart."*

When God chooses to reveal Himself and speak to a person, it is because He intends to do a work *through* that person. God always chooses a man or woman after His own heart. God will accept nothing less than a man or woman who seeks Him with all their heart, all their mind, and all their strength.

Again, it comes down to one of two choices. You will either be *for* God or *against* Him. There is no middle ground. You either believe that He exists and follow His commandments, or you don't.

King David was far from perfect, but he had a heart for God. David loved God and from his youth, he desired and chose to serve him all of his life. When King David sinned against God, he recognized his sin and declared it. He cried out for God's compassion, mercy and forgiveness.

> *BE gracious to me, O God, according to Your lovingkindness; According to the greatness of Your compassion blot out my transgressions. Wash me thoroughly from my iniquity And cleanse me from my sin. For I know my transgressions, And my sin is ever before me. Against You, You only, I have sinned And done what is evil in Your sight, So that You are justified when You speak And blameless when You judge. Psalm 51:1-4*

Do you have a heart for God? What is the condition of your heart toward God? Are you willing to go before Him, humble yourself, and in the greatness of His compassion and mercy, ask that He blot out your transgressions?

Have you sinned against God? Is your sin ever before you? Is it the desire of your heart for God to *wash you thoroughly* from your iniquity and cleanse you from your sin?

Seek the Lord while He is near!

Seek Him, and you *will* find Him. Ask Him, and He *will* cleanse you from your sins. Believe Him, for He is faithful to cleanse you from *all* your unrighteousness, and before Him you *will be clean*!

Like Joshua and like Israel, you are being called this very day to choose whom you will serve.

I pray you will choose God. I pray you will choose to follow Him, to know Him, to obey Him and to be blessed by Him.

I know it's the *best* decision I *ever* made.

CHAPTER 8

ISRAEL - A NATION AGAIN IN THE 20TH CENTURY

Never before in human history has a nation been completely destroyed, its people scattered throughout the nations of the earth for over 2000 years, and then suddenly been brought back to life. Israel's resurrection is nothing short of a miracle and a fulfillment of biblical prophecy.

At the beginning of this book, I mentioned the fact that over 2,500 years ago the prophet, Ezekiel prophesied the restoration of Israel to its land in the last days.

> *Then He said to me, "Son of man, <u>these bones are the whole house of Israel</u>; behold, they say, 'Our bones are dried up and our hope has perished. We are completely cut off.' Therefore, prophesy and say to them, Thus says the Lord GOD, Behold, I will open your graves and cause you to come up out of your graves, My people; <u>and I will bring you into the land of Israel</u>." Ezekiel 37:11-12*

Note that 2,500 years ago the Lord called the name of the land that He would bring them into in the last days, the land of *"Israel"*. This is the land in the Bible that was called the *"land of Canaan."* Yet, the Lord chose to declare that the name of the land in these last days should be called *"the land of Israel"*.

Nowhere in Scripture is the land called "the land of Palestine!"

At the dawn of the 21st century, The United Nations is intent on creating a "Palestinian nation" that is carved out of what God has called "the land of Israel."

This plan reflects the counsel of man, *not* the counsel, wisdom or plan of God!

Modern Israel became a nation in May of 1948, after more than 2,500 years of dispersion. In 1945, as World War II came to an end, the

European Jewish community was almost completely annihilated in Hitler's concentration camps.

Five million Jewish adults and more than one million infants and children met their deaths in Hitler's gas chambers. As the verses in Ezekiel prophesied more than 2500 years before, truly all that was left of European Jewry was dry bones.

Again in Ezekiel, the Lord declared that it was He who removed Israel from the land, and it was He who would bring them back again and would give them *"the land of Israel."*

> *Therefore say, 'Thus says the Lord GOD, 'Though I had removed them far away among the nations and though I had scattered them among the countries, yet I was a sanctuary for them a little while in the countries where they had gone.'" Therefore say, 'Thus says the Lord GOD, 'I will gather you from the peoples and assemble you out of the countries among which you have been scattered, and <u>I will give you the land of Israel</u>.'"*
> *Ezekiel 11:16-17*

Notice it is the Lord who says, "I will gather you from the peoples and assemble you out of the countries among which you have been scattered."

Israel's disobedience resulted in her being removed from the land.

It was the Lord who scattered Israel because of her disobedience. But remember, God's covenant with Israel regarding their inheritance *of* the land was unconditional and irrevocable. However, Israel's right to live *in* the land *was* conditional. It was predicated upon their obedience to God.

Yet, God in His mercy remembered His covenant with Abraham, and the day arrived when the Lord chose to fulfill His prophecy and to give back to the Jews the land of Israel.

Here again, it is important to note that 2,500 years before it took place the Lord said He would bring the Jews back into the land of *"Israel,"* not *"Canaan"* and not *"Palestine"* ... the land of *"Israel."*

But, why May 1948? Why did God choose this as the date of the resurrection of the nation of Israel? Was it just a random date in history, or was it the *exact* date prophesied by the Lord thousands of years before?

In the book of Leviticus, the Lord prophesied how He would punish Israel if they sinned against Him and disobeyed His commandments.

> *'And if by these things you are not turned to Me, but act with hostility against Me, then I will act with hostility against you; and I, even I, will strike you seven times for your sins.' Leviticus 26:23-24*

This is a very strange prophecy, and taken as a verse by itself, it is impossible to understand. However, when we go forward in the Bible to the book of Ezekiel, and examine a prophecy there regarding Israel, we gain some astounding insight into why the resurrection of Israel in May of 1948 was no accident. The Lord commands Ezekiel to do something very strange in Chapter 4.

EZEKIEL IS TOLD TO LIE ON HIS RIGHT SIDE AND THEN ON HIS LEFT SIDE FOR THE NUMBER OF DAYS CORRESPONDING TO THE YEARS OF ISRAEL'S INIQUITY.

> *"As for you lie down on your left side and lay the iniquity of the house of Israel on it; you shall bear their iniquity for the number of days that you lie on it. For I have assigned you a number of days corresponding to the years of their iniquity, three hundred and ninety days; thus you shall bear the iniquity of the house of Israel. When you have completed these, you shall lie down a second time, but on your right side and bear the iniquity of the house of Judah; I have assigned it to you for forty days, a day for each year." Ezekiel 4:4-6*

God commands Ezekiel to lie down first on his left side for 390 days and then on his right side for 40 days for a total of 430 days.

Each day signifies one year of Israel's iniquity toward the God of Israel. One day for one year or 430 years.

61

This is a strange prophecy when it is taken alone, however when we combine the prophecy in Leviticus with this prophecy in Ezekiel, something truly astounding is revealed about the exact year and month of Israel's rebirth as a nation.

ISRAEL BECAME A NATION IN THE EXACT YEAR, AND IN THE EXACT MONTH THAT THE LORD PROPHESIED THEY WOULD THOUSANDS OF YEARS BEFORE IT HAPPENED!

Ezekiel is told to lie on his right side and left side for the number of days corresponding to the years of Israel's iniquity.

EZEKIEL 4:5- LIE ON LEFT SIDE =   390 (YEARS)

EZEKIEL 4:6- LIE ON RIGHT SIDE=   _40_ (YEARS)

THIS EQUALS =   430 (YEARS)

The captivity of Israel in Babylon was exactly 70 years as prophesied by the prophet Jeremiah. (Jeremiah 25:11-12 & 29:10)

By the decree of King Cyrus of Babylon, the Jews were set free from their captivity in the year 538 B.C.E. Since, at their release, they had already served 70 years of the allotted punishment our base year for counting down is the year 538 B.C.E.

430 Years- (minus) 70 years in Captivity= (equals) 360 years of punishment to come.

> *And if by these things you are not turned to Me, but act with hostility against Me, then I will act with hostility against you; and I, even I, will strike you seven times for your sins. Leviticus 26:23-24*

360(years of punishment to come) X 7 (Israel cursed 7 times for her sins)= 2,520 years

2,520 (years) X 360 days (in a *Jewish* calendar year)= 907,200 days

To convert to common years: 907,200 days@ 365 (days per year) = 2,485 years and 5 months (or 2,485.5)

Or

907,200 days/ 365= 2,485 years plus 5 months

2485.5– 538 B.C= 1,947 years and 5 months

There is no "0" year. The end of the *old* year, 1 BC, ushers in the *new* year, 1 AD.

So we call "0" year, year 1. Then in turn, year 1 we call year 2, and so on.

Therefore, the year 1947.5 we call the year 1948.5.

SO 1,947.5 YEARS AFTER 538 BC= THE YEAR 1948.5

MAY IS THE 5TH MONTH OF THE YEAR, AND ON MAY 15th OF 1948 ISRAEL BECAME A NATION AGAIN.

There are no accidents where the Lord is concerned! God's judgments are certain and precise and they have a beginning and an end!

Israel was always a nation in the eyes of the Lord. He prophesied Israel's rebirth again in the book of Isaiah, chapter 66.

> *Who has heard such a thing? Who has seen such things? Can a land be born in one day? Can a nation be brought forth all at once? As soon as Zion travailed, she also brought forth her sons. "Shall I bring to the point of birth and not give delivery?" Says the LORD. "Or shall I who gives delivery shut the womb?" says your God.*
> *Isaiah 66:8-9*

Only the God of all time and eternity could prophesy and bring to pass with such precision and accuracy, in the exact year and in the exact month, the resurrection of a nation after more than 2,500 years of extinction!

CHAPTER 9

IS THERE A GOD IN ISRAEL?

Israel is a nation beset on all sides by Muslim enemies. The United Nations, the European Union, and the Arab nations are all seeking the division and ultimate destruction of the nation of Israel.

This raises some very interesting questions regarding modern Israel.

Is God still involved with His creation? Can God protect what He created?

Can God sustain what His great mind conceived and His great hand set in motion? Can He fulfill His purpose for Israel and for all His creation?

Let there be no doubt that He is, He can and He will.

The God of Israel is El Elyon- God Most High!

THE REBIRTH OF ISRAEL- A NATION BIRTHED IN WAR

Between the time the United Nations voted to create the nation of Israel in November of 1947, and the arrival of the actual date in May 1948, war raged throughout Israel. The British were administering the territory until their mandate expired in May of 1948.

Between December and May, the British began a pull out of their troops and as they withdrew, they gave considerable assistance to the Arabs. The British enforced a naval blockade to keep Jews from entering the land, and this had the effect of not allowing the Jews to bring in arms and ammunition to help them in the coming war.

Meanwhile, the British did nothing to halt the Trans-Jordan Arab Legion, organized, trained and commanded by the British, when they embarked on offensive operations before the British Mandate ended against the Jews.

The War of Liberation began in earnest in April and the Jewish people fought against overwhelming odds. But they were victorious.

"They will fight against you, but they will not overcome you, for I am with you to deliver you," declares the LORD.
Jeremiah 1:19

1948: In the 1948 war of Independence, Israel prevailed. However, one-half of Jerusalem and most of the West Bank remained in Jordanian hands. At the end of this war, Jerusalem was a city surrounded on six sides by the Jordanian's whose territory extended to within twelve miles of Tel Aviv on the coast.

1955: On October 24, 1955, Egypt, Jordan and Syria signed a military pact and the die was cast for the Suez Crisis and the War of 1956.

1956: Egypt began their move to restrict Israeli ships from using the Suez Canal. This became known as the Suez Crisis. Egypt also attempted to seal off the Israeli port of Eilat on the Gulf of Aqaba. Again, Israel prevailed in this war of 1956, but Jerusalem remained in Jordanian hands. Israel held a part of Jerusalem, but Jordan still controlled all of the land around it, and only one narrow road allowed the Jews access to Jerusalem from Tel Aviv.

1967: Only eleven years later in 1967, the same nations joined together with Iraq and Saudi Arabia and attacked Israel in a combined assault. Their battle plan was to cut Israel into 3 parts, with Syria attacking from the Golan Heights in the North, Jordan attacking through Jerusalem into the heart of Israel, and Egypt attacking with its vast army advancing from the south.

This plan had great possibilities for the Jordanians, as the Jordanian border at that time was only twelve miles from Israel's main city, Tel Aviv. A determined force, they reasoned that they could smash across it in short order.

1973: On Yom Kippur, (Jewish Day of Atonement), October 6, 1973, Syria invaded Israel along the Golan Heights border in the north. Simultaneously, Egypt launched an attack across the Suez Canal into the Sinai. A few days later, Jordan and Iraq attack from the East.

Israel was outnumbered in the initial attacks by more than ten to one in tanks and infantry. Once again, Israel was a nation fighting for its life against the Arab nations. Once again, the goal of the Arab nations was the complete destruction of the nation of Israel.

Only by God's grace and His faithfulness, Israel was victorious.

1982: Israel has long sought a peaceful northern border. For Arab residents of south Lebanon, PLO rule was a nightmare. After Arafat's attempt to overthrow the Kingdom of Jordan, Arafat along with the PLO was expelled from Jordan by King Hussein in 1970; many of his cadres followed him to Lebanon. The PLO seized whole areas of the country, where it brutalized the population and usurped Lebanese government authority.

The situation in the Galilee became intolerable for the Israeli's as the frequency of attacks forced thousands of residents to flee their homes or to spend large amounts of time in bomb shelters. Israel was not prepared to wait for more deadly attacks to be launched against its civilian population before acting against the terrorists.

The final provocation occurred in June 1982 when a Palestinian terrorist group led by Abu Nidal attempted to assassinate Israel's Ambassador to Great Britain, Shlomo Argov. The IDF subsequently attacked Lebanon again on June 4-5, 1982. The PLO responded with a massive artillery and mortar attack on the Israeli population of the Galilee. On June 6, the IDF moved into Lebanon to drive out the terrorists in "Operation Peace for Galilee."

The initial success of the Israeli operation led officials to broaden the objective to expel the PLO from Lebanon and induce the country's leaders to sign a peace treaty. In 1983, Lebanon's

President, Amin Gemayel, signed a peace treaty with Israel. A year later, Syria forced Gemayel to renege on the agreement. The war then became drawn out as the IDF captured Beirut and surrounded Yasser Arafat and his guerrillas.

Most of the terrorist groups that threaten Israel have not been disarmed. For example, thousands of terrorists currently in Lebanon are members of Hezbullah. The group receives financial support and arms from Iran, usually via Damascus. Today, Hezbullah now has over 8,000 Katyusha rockets aimed at northern Israel, and continues to fire artillery shells into the northern Galilee.

Israel pulled all its troops out of southern Lebanon on May 24, 2000, ending a 22-year military presence there. All of Israel's Defense Forces and South Lebanon Army outposts were evacuated. The Israeli withdrawal was conducted in coordination with the UN, and constituted an Israeli fulfillment of its obligations under Security Council Resolution 425 (1978).

1991: Iraq had one of the largest and most powerful armies in the world prior to its invasion of Kuwait. None of the Gulf States could have challenged the Iraqis without direct U.S. intervention. When Iraq invaded Kuwait in 1991, the United States and its allies reacted quickly knowing that Saddam's goal was not just Kuwait, but Saudi Arabia.

When the United States coalition forces launched a counter attack against Iraq, Israel was not allowed to join the coalition forces. However, it was not long before Saddam began to rain down Scud Missiles on Israeli cities. The damage caused by the 39 Iraqi Scud missiles that landed in Tel Aviv and Haifa was extensive. Approximately 3,300 apartments and other buildings were affected in the greater Tel Aviv area.

The biggest cost was in human lives. A total of 74 people died as a consequence of Scud attacks. Two died in direct hits, four from suffocation in gas masks and the rest from heart attacks (*Jerusalem Post*, January 17, 1992).

2000: In July of 2000, Yasser Arafat staged his walk out of the Camp David peace talks and began to implement his plans for the armed struggle to destroy Israel.

On September 28, 2000, Ariel Sharon visited the Temple Mount in Jerusalem. This visit became the pretext for instigating large scale demonstrations, the start of the Al-Aqsa intifada. In a revealing interview with the London-based Arabic daily Al-Hayat (September 29, 2001), Marwan Barghouti, head of the Tanzim, admitted his critical role in igniting the October 2000 intifada in both the West Bank and Gaza, as well as among the Israeli Arabs:

I knew that the end of September was the last period (of time) before the explosion, but when Sharon reached the Al-Aqsa Mosque, this was the most appropriate moment for the outbreak of the intifada

Since Arafat launched his Intifada in September 2000, hundreds of Israeli's have been killed, and thousands injured along with similar numbers on the Palestinian side. The commencement of the Intifada revealed that Arafat's plans had nothing to do with peace. His plans had nothing to do with exchanging land for peace. His goal was the same as the Arab nations, the complete destruction of the State of Israel.

The prophecy of Psalm 83 declares the plan of Arafat and the Arab nations are they are being fulfilled as we write this book.

O GOD, do not remain quiet; Do not be silent and, O God, do not be still. For behold, Your enemies make an uproar, And those who hate You have exalted themselves. They make shrewd plans against Your people, And conspire together against Your treasured ones. Psalm 83:1-4

In 1948, 1956, 1967, and again in 1973, the Arabs sought the complete annihilation of the state of Israel. In many cases, Israel was outnumbered by more than 10 to 1. How did Israel survive against such overwhelming odds?

What the Arabs did not understand was they had not just declared war against Israel and the Jewish people. In reality, they had declared war against the God of Israel, as well.

> "Then I will make you to this people a fortified wall of bronze; And though they fight against you, they will not prevail over you; For I am with you to save you and deliver you," declares the LORD. Jeremiah 15:20

The God of Israel is well able to defend that which He created. Still today, the Arab nations seek the complete destruction of the nation of Israel and having conspired together, they have made a covenant *against* the Lord God of Israel.

> They, (the Arab nations) have said, "Come, and let us wipe them out as a nation, That the name of Israel be remembered no more." For they have conspired together with one mind; Against You they make a covenant. Psalm 83:4-5

These prophetic verses, written so long ago yet so concurrent with today's headlines, contain the heart and soul of the Israeli, Arab and Palestinian conflict. The world believes this conflict is all about peace. However, and contrary to popular belief, the situation in the Middle East has nothing whatsoever to do with peace. The plans and the purpose of the Arab nations is not peace. It never has been, and never will be.

The plan and purpose of the Arab nations is the complete destruction of the State of Israel. The Bible declares it because it's true. God revealed this truth to the Psalmist Asaph, and moved upon him to record it in order to give those who lack understanding of the deeper issues at work here ... the lies and deception masked by talks of peace ... and true understanding.

This conflict didn't just start. This conflict began thousands of years ago, and it is still raging. There will never be peace in the Middle East because it is a *spiritual* battle in which the Arab and Palestinian God of Islam has declared war on the God of Israel. The list is nearly endless of those who have tried to bring peace to the Middle East. The United Nations, the European Union, the United States, Presidents,

Prime Ministers, Foreign Ministers, Kings, Princes, Secretaries of State and the membership goes on. Why have they all failed?

They have all failed because they do not understand the basis of this conflict. They are trying to solve this strife based upon limited and flawed human wisdom, *not* the infinite wisdom and eternal plan of God for Israel in these last days. Their solution is the division of the land of Israel, the division of Jerusalem, and the creation of a Muslim terrorist state on the land promised to Israel by God.

The plans and schemes of man will always fail when it comes to Israel, because no one can thwart the plan of God.

All of the nations who are lining up against this tiny nation of Israel do not understand that while Israel is small, the God of Israel is not!

The nations are asking the same question today that Pharaoh of Egypt asked Moses.

> *But Pharaoh said, "Who is the LORD that I should obey His voice to let Israel go? I do not know the LORD, and besides, I will not let Israel go." Exodus 5:2*

To this very day, the nations still do not understand that when they make war against Israel, they are making war against the God of Israel. All the nations of the earth should know that there is a God in Israel to whom His people have always turned in times of conflict and warfare. And He has never failed them.

His name is Adonai Sabaoth. In Hebrew, the word "Sabaoth" means "mass." In this sense, it means a mass of heavenly beings, a mass of angels, or an army of heavenly hosts.

Like Pharaoh, who discovered too late, the days are coming when all the nations will come to know Adonai Sabaoth and that He is the God of Israel.

God does not change! Adonai Sabaoth protects Israel because He is a covenant keeping God. Allah is not god, and he is certainly not the god of Israel. Whenever Allah and his agents contend with the God of Israel, they will always fail.

All the nations of the earth will come to understand in the last days that the Lord God of Israel is the one who fights for Israel against her enemies. No army, no kingdom, no power, no principality can prevail against Adonai Sabaoth, the Lord of Hosts, the God of Israel.

In days long ago the Lord instructed Israel what to do when they approached the battle against their enemies.

> *When you are approaching the battle, the priest shall come near and speak to the people. He shall say to them, "Hear, O Israel, you are approaching the battle against your enemies today. Do not be fainthearted. Do not be afraid, or panic, or tremble before them, for the LORD your God is the one who goes with you, to fight for you against your enemies, to save you." Deuteronomy 20:2-4*

Adonai Sabaoth rules over and is Lord over all powers, principalities, and rulers in heaven and on earth. Adonai Sabaoth is the Lord of Hosts!

Adonai Sabaoth is the name that David called upon when he stood alone against the Philistine giant, Goliath. David, a young shepherd boy found himself standing with a slingshot in the shadow of a nine-foot giant armed with sword, spear, shield and full body armor!

> *When the Philistine looked and saw David, he disdained him; for he was but a youth, and ruddy, with a handsome appearance. The Philistine said to David, "Am I a dog, that you come to me with sticks?" And the Philistine cursed David by his gods. The Philistine also said to David, "Come to me, and I will give your flesh to the birds of the sky and the beasts of the field." I Samuel 17:42-44*

Listen now to David's reply to the one who mocked Adonai Sabaoth, the Lord of Hosts.

Then David said to the Philistine, "You come to me with a sword, a spear, and a javelin, but I come to you in the name of the LORD of hosts, the God of the armies of Israel, whom you have taunted. This day the LORD will deliver you up into my hands, and I will strike you down and remove your head from you. And I will give the dead bodies of the army of the Philistines this day to the birds of the sky and the wild beasts of the earth, that all the earth may know that there is a God in Israel and that all this assembly may know that the LORD does not deliver by sword or by spear; for the battle is the LORD'S and He will give you into our hands." I Samuel 17:45-47

The battle is the Lord's! And just as in the day when David faced Goliath, every time the Arab armies come against Israel they are coming against the <u>God of Israel</u>, <u>Adonai Sabaoth</u>, <u>and the Lord of Hosts!</u>

Against the combined attack of armies and air forces of Egypt, Jordan, Syria, Iraq and Saudi Arabia, Adonai Sabaoth went before the vastly outnumbered army of Israel. Incredibly, Jerusalem fell to the army of Israel and in 1967, came under Israeli control for the first time in over 2,500 years!

How was this possible?

It was *only* possible because the God of Israel, Adonai Sabaoth, who had promised in His word that He will, went before the army of Israel. It was the Lord's battle, as he fought for His city, His people, His land and His covenant to prove one simple point; there is a God in Israel and His name is Adonai Sabaoth – the Lord of Hosts.

It was the Lord of Hosts who delivered Jerusalem into Israel's hands! He delivered His holy city out of the hands of the God of Islam and into the hands of the God of Israel.

The Lord reminded the world that He had not forgotten Jerusalem. It is His eternal city and in which He intends one day to dwell with His chosen people Israel!

If I forget you, O Jerusalem, may my right hand forget her skill. May My tongue cling to the roof of my mouth if I do not remember you, if I do not exalt Jerusalem above my chief joy. Psalm 137:5-6

And God does not change!

CHAPTER 10

GOD'S COMMANDMENTS ARE ETERNAL

The Lord gave the land to Israel to confirm His covenant with Abraham. Throughout Israel's modern day history, whenever the enemies of the God of Israel attacked her, He defended her and Israel always emerged victorious.

However, the Lord gave Israel's leaders and the people specific instructions on what they were to do when they entered the land of Israel during the time of Joshua.

The Lord revealed to them that He would drive out the nations from before them only when Israel's leaders obeyed His specific commandments regarding the inhabitants of the land and their gods.

The Lord was very clear on these two issues, and we read in Exodus 34 how He chastised Israel after Joshua's death for their disobedience.

> *"Watch yourself that you make <u>no covenant with the inhabitants</u> of the land into which you are going, or <u>it will become a snare in your midst</u>. But rather, you are to <u>tear down their altars and smash their sacred pillars and cut down their Asherim (wooden symbols of the female deity, Asherah)</u>; for you shall not worship any other god, for the LORD, whose name is Jealous, is a jealous God; otherwise you might make a covenant with the inhabitants of the land and they would play the harlot with their gods and sacrifice to their gods, and someone might invite you to eat of his sacrifice." Exodus 34:12-15*

Incredibly, in 1967, when God delivered Jerusalem into the hands of Israel's after 2,500 years of captivity, Israel's leaders chose *not* to obey the commandment of the Lord *"to tear down the altars"* to other gods in their midst.

Israel did not tear down the greatest altar to a foreign god in their midst. The Al-Aksa Mosque still sits atop the Temple Mount, in the very heart of Jerusalem's Old City.

The Lord declared to Israel,

> *"You shall have no other gods before Me!" Exodus 20:3*
> *"...For the LORD, whose name is jealous, is a jealous God."*
> *Exodus 34:14*

The Lord commanded the Israelites to have no other gods before them or in their midst, because the God of Israel is a jealous God. The Lord knew that a monument, altar or idol to a foreign god would be a snare to His people.

The god of Islam is not the God of Israel. Allah is a foreign god. And the house of Allah, the mosque with the gold dome, sits atop the Mountain of God in the very heart of Jerusalem today.

Why did Israel disobey the Lord? Israel disobeyed the Lord because they wanted to please the nations rather than follow the commandments of their God.

> *Thus you will know that I am the LORD; for you have not walked in My statutes nor have you executed My ordinances, but have acted according to the ordinances of the nations around you. Ezekiel 11:12*

Israel sought to do what was right in the eyes of the nations and in the eyes of man, and was disobedient to God's commandment to destroy the idol and place of worship to a foreign god in the midst of Jerusalem.

The mosque with the gold dome stands today as a glaring monument to modern day Israel's disobedience to the commandments of their God; to destroy all idols and places of worship to a foreign god in their midst.

GOD DOES NOT CHANGE

In the days when Israel was ruled by the Judges, they paid a heavy price for their disobedience in allowing other gods in their midst.

Today, as in the time of Judges, Israel is once again paying a very heavy price for her disobedience. The Lord declared to Israel exactly what would happen to them if they did not destroy the altars of the foreign gods in their midst.

> *Know with certainty that the LORD your God will not continue to drive these nations out from before you; but they will be a snare and a trap to you, and a whip on your sides and thorns in your eyes, until you perish from off this good land which the LORD your God has given you. Joshua 23:13*

Just as God's covenant with Abraham was everlasting, so are His commandments everlasting. What the Lord declared to Israel 3,500 years ago has not changed.

Because of Israel's disobedience, and just as God said they would, the Palestinians who worship the god of Islam have truly *become a snare and a thorn in the sides of all Israel.*

Disobedience to God has proven to be very costly for Israel. It was in the time of Moses and Joshua and it is so today. It has not and will not change because the God of Abraham is the same yesterday, today, and tomorrow.

THE CONSEQUENCES OF DISOBEDIENCE TO GOD HAVE NOT CHANGED

Because of Israel's disobedience, the Lord God of Israel did *not* drive out the Palestinians, and they are a thorn in Israel's side to this very day.

Because Israel chose not to obey God and destroy the Mosque with the gold dome, every Friday horrible tirades against Israel, the Jewish people, and Americans are preached to the Muslims from the Al-Aksa Mosque in the heart of Jerusalem.

To the Arab, a Jew is a Jew, whether he lives in Israel or America. A good example of these tirades against America and American Jews was delivered by the Palestinian Authority leader, Mufti Ikrama Sabri in his weekly prayer sermon at Al-Aksa Mosque on the Temple Mount, as broadcast live by The Voice of Palestine on Friday, July 11, 1997.

"OH, ALLAH -- DESTROY AMERICA!

For she is ruled by Zionist Jews! Allah shall take revenge on behalf of his prophet against the colonialist settlers who are sons of monkeys and pigs! Forgive us, Mohammad, for the acts of these sons of monkeys and pigs, who sought to harm your sanctity."

This is an example of the heart and soul, of the intense hatred the Palestinians and those who worship Allah have toward Jews-all Jews-everywhere. Not just, as some might believe, only toward those with whom they share a plot of land.

The following excerpt is from a message that was given on Palestinian TV and aired on August 3, 2001.

"I heard a youth say, 'Oh, Sheikh, I am now 14 years old. I have 4 more years and then I will go to blow myself up among Allah's enemies. I will blow myself up among the Jews.' I said to him, 'Allah should let you merit martyrdom and let me merit martyrdom'."

"All weapons must be aimed at the Jews, at the enemies of Allah, the cursed nation in the Koran, whom the Koran describes as monkeys and pigs, worshippers of the calf and idol worshippers."

"Allah shall make the Moslem rule over the Jew, we will blow them up in Hadera, we will blow them up in Tel-Aviv and in Netanya in the righteousness of Allah against this riff-raff, we will fight against them and rule over them until the Jew will hide behind the trees and stones and the tree and stone will say: 'Moslem! Servant of Allah, there is a Jew behind me. Kill him!"

"We will enter Jerusalem as conquerors, and Jaffa as conquerors, and Haifa as conquerors and Ashkelon as conquerors! We are certain that the victory is quickly coming! As we bless anyone who rises against a soldier, we bless all those who educate their children to Jihad and to martyrdom! Blessings to he who shot a bullet into the head of a Jew!"

It is crystal clear why there is no peace in the Middle East! Arafat and the Arab nations do not want peace. They want all of Israel. And they want the death of all Jews. Hardly a prescription for peace!

ISRAEL'S FALSE SHEPHERDS

Can anyone imagine the God of Abraham telling King David to bring the king of the Philistines to Jerusalem and to divide it for the sole purpose of establishing a capital for a "foreign god?"

Can anyone imagine the Lord telling King David, "Go and divide the land I promised Israel by covenant and give it over to the Philistines? Divide the land so the Philistines can establish a new nation in the midst of Israel?"

If the God of Israel did this, He would not be the God of Israel! The Lord commanded Israel to *possess* the land. He *never* commanded them to "divide it" or "give it over" to those who worship a foreign god.

> *'Hence I have said to you, "You are to possess their land, and I Myself will give it to you to possess it, a land flowing with milk and honey." I am the LORD your God, who has separated you from the peoples.' Leviticus 20:24*

Yet, Israel has sought to follow the wisdom of man and *not* the wisdom and commandments of the God of Israel.

For seven years, the shepherds (leaders) of Israel have followed the wisdom of the world and embraced the Oslo Peace Process. For seven years, they have espoused the idea that Israel can make a covenant with the enemies of the God of Abraham, Isaac and Jacob and there will be peace. And God declares the exact opposite.

> *"Make <u>no covenant</u> with the inhabitants of the land ... or <u>it will become a snare in your midst</u>." Exodus 34:12*

The architects of Oslo, the *"supposed"* shepherds of Israel have led the people of Israel down a path declaring, *"Peace! Peace!"*

Instead of peace, the shepherds of Israel have led their people down a road to violence, war and terror. This "peace process" had nothing to do with peace. That is exactly why it has failed. And that is why it has led to war, terror and death for thousands of Israeli's and Palestinians.

The wisdom and plans of men are seeking to thwart the plan of God for Israel in these last days. Their plans will not prevail, because they are not of God.

BEWARE SHEPHERDS OF ISRAEL WHO SEEK TO MAKE A COVENANT WITH THE INHABITANTS OF THE LAND

"It will come about at that time that I will search Jerusalem with lamps, And I will punish the men who are stagnant in spirit, who say in their hearts, 'the LORD will not do good or evil!'" Zephaniah 1:12

Woe to the shepherds of Israel who say, *"The Lord will do no good or evil!"*

Woe to the shepherds of Israel who say, *"Peace! Peace!"* but there is no peace!

"They heal the brokenness of the daughter of My people superficially, Saying, 'Peace, peace,' But there is no peace." Jeremiah 8:11

Woe to the nations who demand that Israel make a covenant with the inhabitants of the land, to divide it and create a nation who worships a foreign god!

Woe to the nations who demand the division of Jerusalem, and seek to create a capital to a foreign god!

What does Adonai Sabaoth say to them on this matter?

The LORD nullifies the counsel of the nations; He frustrates the plans of the peoples. The counsel of the LORD stands forever, The plans of His heart from generation to generation. Blessed is the nation whose God is the LORD, the people whom He has chosen for His own inheritance. Psalm 33:10-12

CHAPTER 11

GOD OF ISRAEL-A COVENANT KEEPING GOD

The God of Israel is a covenant keeping God that places the integrity of His word, as written in the Bible, above even His own name. Either God's word is true or it is not. Here again, we are faced with a choice. Either we choose to believe God and base our faith upon His word, the Bible, or we choose not to.

Many people seek proof that God exists. To them we say, "Read and study His word regarding Israel, and you will *know* there is a God in Israel."

The Bible is the only book ever written that *accurately* predicts hundreds of events that will take place thousands of years after the prophecy is written. No other book can make that claim.

There are 39 chapters in the Old Testament, and 27 chapters in the New Testament. The Bible contains 66 books written by many different authors over thousand of years; yet they have one central theme.

The theme is the coming of the Messiah to rule and reign on the earth. There are many prophecies that are written about what will take place before His return. One of the most significant is the re-gathering of the Jews from the land of the north, the former Soviet Union."

I WILL BRING UP YOUR SONS FROM THE LAND OF THE NORTH

Until 1989, it was impossible for Jews from the Soviet Union to immigrate to Israel. Jews came to Israel from all the other nations of the world, but not from the Soviet Union.

The Russians had a name for and branded the Jews who sought to emigrate from the Soviet Union to Israel. They called them "Refusenicks."

Jews wanting to emigrate from Russia were put into prison, denied work, persecuted, sent off to Siberia and many were even murdered. Over 300,000 Soviet Jews applied for visas to immigrate to Israel and all were denied exit visas by the Soviet Union.

Just as the Egyptian Pharaoh had refused to let the children of Israel go but instead kept them in bondage and slavery, the Soviet Union refused to allow any of the remaining 2.7 million Russian Jews to leave and immigrate to Israel. The Lord was once again saying to a powerful and mighty nation, "Let My people go!"

The Lord had prophesied 2,500 years earlier that He would bring His people "from the land of the north to the land of Israel", and the fulfillment of this prophecy began in 1989 with nothing less than the collapse of the former Soviet Union.

God had determined that the day and the hour had arrived when He, as He had promised, would restore them to their own land.

The news of the collapse of the Soviet Union stunned the entire world! How many of you reading this, remember that day? Who would have *ever* believed that the massive former Soviet Union would collapse and be divided into many nations? This mighty and powerful nation that threatened the world with annihilation for more than fifty years, crumbled and collapsed without a single shot being fired. Unbelievable! Yet true.

Many Americans claimed "democracy" had brought down the former Soviet Union. American democracy did not bring down the former Soviet Union, the Lord God of Israel did in order to fulfill His prophecy and His purpose for Israel as recorded more than two thousand five hundred years ago!

GOD IS FAITHFUL TO HIS WORD

We are writing this book today so that you will understand how completely faithful God is to His word. What He promises in His word, the Bible, *will* come to pass whether we believe and accept it or not. It is the Lord God of Israel who brought down the former Soviet Union and He did it for one specific purpose- *to fulfill biblical prophecy regarding the Jews.*

Hear the word of the LORD, O nations, and declare in the coastlands afar off, and say, "He who scattered Israel will gather him and keep him as a shepherd keeps his flock."
Jeremiah 31:10

God's purpose was to re-gather His people from the "land of the North".

"Therefore behold, days are coming," declares the LORD, "when it will no longer be said, 'As the LORD lives, who brought up the sons of Israel out of the land of Egypt,' but, 'As the LORD lives, who brought up the sons of Israel from the land of the north and from all the countries where He had banished them.' For I will restore them to their own land which I gave to their fathers."
Jeremiah 16:14-15

Unlike the first Exodus that brought the Jews out of Egypt, the Lord declared the second Exodus would be so dramatic that the Jews will speak of it as *greater* than the first one under Moses.

"Therefore behold, the days are coming," declares the LORD, "when they will no longer say, 'As the LORD lives, who brought up the sons of Israel from the land of Egypt,' but, 'As the LORD lives, who brought up and led back the descendants of the household of Israel from the north land and from all the countries where I had driven them.' Then they will live on their own soil." Jeremiah 23:7-8

Was any nation, other than America, equal or greater in military power than the former Soviet Union? Was not Communism the primary force sweeping the world, forcing nations and peoples into subjugation under their cruel hand? For more than forty years the United States and Europe spent hundreds of billions of dollars on defense for one single purpose, to prepare for a war with the former Soviet Union.

Yet, the once mighty military empire collapsed without a single bullet being expended. Why? The former Soviet Union collapsed because, like Pharaoh, they chose not to know nor obey the God in Israel.

Like Pharaoh, the Soviet Union said to the Jews seeking to immigrate to Israel,

> .... *"Who is the LORD that I should obey His voice to let Israel go? I do not know the LORD, and besides, I will not let Israel go."*
> *Exodus 5:2*

Just as in the days of Pharaoh when the Lord took the Jews out of Egypt, beginning in 1989 with the collapse of the Soviet Union, the Lord began bringing the Jews from "the land of the north," to Israel. Just as the Lord had said, *"Then they will live on their own soil!"*

Biblical prophecy, when confirmed in human history, is living proof that there is a God in Israel and that His Word is true. Imbedded in these verses is another truth that is often overlooked. The Lord said, *"As I live!"*

The God of Israel is the *living* God!

THE LORD IS ISRAEL'S SHEPHERD

> *For thus says the Lord GOD, "Behold, I Myself will search for My sheep and seek them out. As a shepherd cares for his herd in the day when he is among his scattered sheep, so I will care for My sheep and will deliver them from all the places to which they were scattered on a cloudy and gloomy day. I will bring them out from the peoples and gather them from the countries and bring them to their own land; and I will feed them on the mountains of Israel, by the streams, and in all the inhabited places of the land. I will feed My flock and I will lead them to rest," declares the Lord GOD. I will seek the lost, bring back the scattered, bind up the broken and strengthen the sick...."*
> *Ezekiel 34:11-13, 15-16*

In Hebrew, the name of the Lord who is the Shepherd of Israel is Adonai Ro'i.

Just as the word of God declared, thousands of years before it took place, Adonai Ro'i, the Shepherd of Israel, searched for His lost sheep. He sought them out. He found them in "the land of the north" and He led them back to the mountains of Israel. The Lord said it, and the Lord is doing it!

In 1989, the only nation directly north of Jerusalem that was filled with Jews was the Soviet Union. Since 1989, more than one million Jews have come from all parts of the former Soviet Union to become Israeli citizens. And, as we write this book, there are still thousands coming every month from "the land of the north."

This incredible prophecy, written thousands of years ago, has come to pass right before our very eyes and the eyes of the world. It was not a hidden event. It was manifested plainly and clearly so that the entire world could see and know that the living God of Israel keeps His Word.

Yet, the Arab nations, the European Union and the United Nations have consistently sought the destruction of the nation of Israel. What does the Word of God say regarding these nations?

> *Behold, the nations count as a drop in the bucket, as dust on the scales; the coastlands weigh no more than powder. Isaiah 40:15*

Adonai Ro'i, the Lord who is the Shepherd of Israel said, "I will bring them back into the land of Israel." God said it, and God is doing it. Why did the Lord perform this great miracle?

> *"Then they will know that I am the Lord their God..." Ezekiel 39:28*

NOT ONLY FROM THE LAND OF THE NORTH

> *When I bring them back from the peoples and gather them from the lands of their enemies, then I shall be sanctified through them in the sight of the many nations. Then they will know that I am the LORD their God because I made them go into exile among the nations, and then gathered them again to their own land; and I will leave none of them there any longer. Ezekiel 39:27-28*

Notice the Lord declared, "When I bring them back from the peoples and gather them from the lands of their enemies ... I will leave none of them there any longer."

None means exactly what the Lord declared – none. Not a single Jew will be left.

Why will the Lord do this great thing?

> *"Then they will know that I am the Lord their God..."*
> *Ezekiel 39:28*

This is a difficult concept for the American Jew to grasp. It was a difficult concept for the Jews living in Argentina to grasp until December of 2001 when the government, economy and economic system of Argentina collapsed. Suddenly, everything they owned was worthless.

It is sad that they did not understand or believe the word of the Lord when He said, "NONE of them will be left."

Today, thousands of Jews are lining up to immigrate to Israel from Argentina. And believe it or not, the day is coming when the Jews of America will flee to Israel just as Jews have fled from the former Soviet Union and Argentina.

Anti-Semitism is rearing its ugly head in France, England, Germany, the former Soviet Union, and many parts of Europe just as it did in the days of Hitler! Is the rest of the world so far behind?

God said NONE of them will be left behind, which can be interpreted to mean ALL of them will be re-gathered.

American Jews are not exempt from God's word. They are an indispensable part of ALL of them.

THE FISHERMEN AND THE HUNTERS

"Behold, I am going to send for many fishermen," declares the LORD, "and they will fish for them; and afterwards I will send for many hunters, and they will hunt them from every mountain and every hill and from the clefts of the rocks." Jeremiah 16:16

Since 1989, there have been many "fishermen" fishing for Jews in the former Soviet Union. There are now "fishermen" in Argentina, France, Germany, England, Europe, and many other nations fishing for Jews to bring them back to Israel.

Every good sportsman knows there is a season for "fishing". When *this* "fishing" season passes the "hunting" season will begin. The day is coming when the Jews of America will be "hunted" and, whether they know and believe the word of the Lord or not, they will flee for their lives because the Lord said, "I will leave none of them there any longer."

As of this writing, it is still the season of "fishing" when Jews can come to Israel and bring their wealth and their possessions with them. But this season *will* pass and the days are coming when they will be "hunted" and will praise God for just allowing them to escape with their lives.

THE LAND OF ISRAEL WILL BECOME LIKE A GARDEN OF EDEN

God continues to fulfill His word regarding the land of Israel by bringing forth yet another miracle. It has been the re-cultivation and rebuilding of the land of Israel.

"The desolate land will be cultivated, instead of being desolation in the sight of everyone who passes by. They will say, 'This desolate land has become like the Garden of Eden; and the waste, desolate and ruined cities are fortified and inhabited.' Then the nations that are left round about you will know that I, the LORD, have rebuilt the ruined places and planted that which was desolate; I, the LORD, have spoken and will do it." Ezekiel 36:34-36

87

The Turks ruled in the land of Israel from 1718 to 1918. During their 200 years of Muslim rule, they turned the land of Israel into a land of deserts and swamps. The Turks instituted a "tree tax" on all the land in Israel. This tax was based upon the number of trees a person had on his land. The more trees he had, the greater the tax. Consequently, the trees were systematically cut down and the land of Israel became a barren desert filled with swamps, mosquitoes and malaria. It had become a land that was completely and utterly desolate.

Yet, the Lord said that Israel would be like the Garden of Eden and His Word never fails.

Beginning in 1948, and in just *fifty-four short years*, the utterly desolate land of Israel has become like a Garden of Eden! The desolate and ruined cities have been rebuilt, fortified and are inhabited by Jews from more than fifty countries around the world!

> *In the days to come Jacob will take root, Israel will blossom and sprout, and they will fill the whole world with fruit. Isaiah 27:6*

Today, the land of Israel, a nation smaller in size than the state of New Jersey, is the third largest exporter of fruit on earth! Just as the Lord prophesied, they are filling the whole world with their fruit! God said it, and just as He declared He would, He has done it!

The nations that are all around Israel know that it was the God of Israel who caused the land to blossom and the ruined places to be rebuilt. That is why they are so angry.

It was not Allah who prophesied these great and wondrous things. It was Adonai Sabaoth, the God of Israel!

It was not Allah who spoke and these great and wondrous things came to pass. It was Adonai Sabaoth, the Lord of Hosts!

> *"I, the Lord have spoken and will do it." Ezekiel 36:36*

Indeed, the desolate land has been cultivated and has become like a Garden of Eden!

Indeed, the cities that were wasted, desolate and ruined are fortified and inhabited!

Indeed, more than 2500 years ago the Lord God of Israel spoke it and is today, doing it!

What the Lord has declared regarding the land of Israel will come to pass.

> *"It is I who have declared and saved and proclaimed, and there was no strange god among you; So you are My witnesses," declares the LORD, "And I am God. Even from eternity I am He And there is none who can deliver out of My hand; I act and who can reverse it?" Isaiah 43:12-13*

The Lord said it, and the world is witness to the fact that He is doing it!

CHAPTER 12

THE BATTLE FOR JERUSALEM AND THE TEMPLE MOUNT

In October of 2000, the Intifada, or Palestinian war against Israel was in full swing. Israeli Prime Minister Ehud Barak, President Bill Clinton, Yasser Arafat, Madeline Albright and Dennis Ross were all busy making plans "to divide Jerusalem, create a Palestinian nation, and to make East Jerusalem the capital of the new Palestinian State."

Not one of these leaders believed or took into account God's covenant with Israel. They did not know the God of Israel nor believe His Word. And because they did not know the God of Israel they said to themselves,

> *"The Lord will not do good or evil!" Zephaniah 1:12*

Because these leaders did not know or fear the God of Israel, it was easy for them to propose one of the greatest abominations of the 20th Century.

Together, they proposed to make a covenant with Yasser Arafat to cede control of East Jerusalem and the Temple Mount, the holiest site in all of Israel and Christendom, to Arafat, the Muslim Palestinians and the god of Islam!

Incredibly, the shepherds of Israel offered to make a covenant with the inhabitants of the land who worshiped a foreign god – Allah. Together they agreed to divide Jerusalem, the city of God, and make it the capital of a new Muslim terrorist nation.

> *Therefore, hear the word of the Lord, O scoffers, Who rule this people who are in Jerusalem, Because you have said, "We have made a covenant with death, And with Sheol we have made a pact. The overwhelming scourge will not reach us when it passes by, For we have made falsehood our refuge and we have concealed ourselves with deception."*

"Your covenant with death will be canceled, And your pact with Sheol will not stand; When the overwhelming scourge passes through, Then you become its trampling place. Isaiah 28:14-15, 18

At each and every meeting, President Clinton pressured Barak to make greater and greater concessions to the Palestinians. However, the more concessions Barak made, the greater the intensity and violence of the attacks against Israel by Arafat and his army of terrorists became.

The leaders of Israel were saying "Peace! Peace!" Yet, there was no peace. There was only war, death, violence and terror for all Israel.

The word of the Lord from Jeremiah, Chapter 8 became a living reality to all Israelis.

"They heal the brokenness of the daughter of My people superficially saying, ' Peace, peace,' But there is no peace." Jeremiah 8:11

Could you ever imagine the God of Israel instructing His shepherd, King David, to bring the king of the Philistines to Jerusalem and say to him, "Take the Old City? Take the Temple Mount! Make it your capital!"

Nowhere in Scripture does the Lord God of Israel command any Israeli leader to say to those who worship a foreign god, "Here is Jerusalem! Take it! Take all this and all that I will give you in order to create a Muslim nation in the midst of the land of Israel!"

Thus says the Lord of hosts, "Behold, I am going to save My people from the land of the east and from the land of the west; and I will bring them back and they will live in the midst of Jerusalem; and they shall be My people, and I will be their God in truth and righteousness." Zechariah 8:7-8

The plan of God for His people and for the city of Jerusalem is very clear in these verses. He redeemed the city of Jerusalem from the hands of the Muslims in 1967 after thousands of years of subjugation.

His plan and purpose in delivering Jerusalem into the hands of Israel was specific.

He declared that He would "*bring His people back*," that "*they will live in the midst of Jerusalem*," that "*they shall be His people*," and that "*He shall be their God.*"

Yet, these leaders, who do not know the God of Israel nor will they obey Him, hatched like the eggs of an adder, *their* plans for Jerusalem in early December of 2000. Barak, Clinton, Albright and Ross offered Arafat control of all East Jerusalem, including two thirds of the Old City, control and sovereignty over the Temple Mount and the Mount of Olives, and to make East Jerusalem Arafat's capital for the new Palestinian State.

The leaders of Israel and America had together spurned God, spurned His Word and spurned His covenant as they laid the holiest sites in the land of Israel and the great City of Jerusalem on the altar of sacrifice to a foreign god.

Can you imagine the turmoil in our hearts as we witnessed Israeli and American leaders turn completely away from God and His covenant with Israel, and in their arrogance, do what was right in their *own* eyes, and in the eyes of the world?

THE HEART OF THE BATTLE IS FOR CONTROL OF THE TEMPLE MOUNT

The Temple Mount is the place where God tested Abraham's obedience by commanding him to bring his only son Isaac, whom he loved, to be offered up as a sacrifice.

The Temple Mount is the place where Solomon built the first temple and the glory of the Lord filled it, and it is the place where Zerubbabel built the second.

The Temple Mount is the place where for more than 2,000 years Jews dispersed throughout the world had turned toward daily and prayed yearningly, "Next year in Jerusalem!" Now this was to be ceded to the god of Islam.

The Temple Mount is the same place where some 2,000 years after Abraham offered up Isaac, the New Testament declares Jesus came to walk, to teach, to touch and to heal and where He was betrayed, beaten and crucified.

Incredibly, the leaders of the government of Israel at the urging of the President of the United States were prepared to offer up this same Temple Mount, the holiest site in all of Israel and Christendom, to the god of Islam!

We shook our heads in disbelief that any Israeli leader would offer to divide Jerusalem, and give up sovereignty of the Old City and the Temple Mount. We found it unbelievable that a U.S. President, representing a self-proclaimed Christian nation, would seek to divide God's holiest city and give it over to the god of Islam.

We found it impossible to believe that the God of Israel would allow Jerusalem to be divided to create the capital of a new Muslim nation. We could not find anywhere in Scripture where God commanded an Israeli leader to return sovereignty of His holy mountain to the control of a foreign god.

Remember, the Lord commanded the children of Israel to *possess* the land as an *everlasting* possession. In every dictionary we've seen, to possess does *not* mean to give away.

ISRAEL'S LEADERS DO NOT KNOW THEIR GOD

We asked ourselves, what kind of men *were* these Israeli leaders who turned a blind eye to 2,000 years of Jewish dispersion?

We asked ourselves, what *kind* of men were these Israeli leaders who sought to revoke God's covenant with Israel by dividing the land God had promised to them as an everlasting possession.

We asked ourselves, what kind of men where these Israeli leaders who could even *consider* ceding the holiest sight in all of Israel, the Temple Mount, to the god of Islam?

We asked ourselves, what kind of men were these Israeli leaders who could *ever* consider dividing Jerusalem, the eternal capital of Israel, in order to create a capital to a foreign god?

We found that all of our questions had the same answer.

These men were Israeli's who did not know the God of Israel. The counselors and advisers of Ehud Barak were men who did not know their God and did not believe in His covenant promises or in His faithfulness to His word!

Yet, what did the Lord God of Israel say about the plans of men and the counsel of nations regarding Jerusalem and Israel?

> *The Lord nullifies the counsel of the nations; He frustrates the plans of the peoples. The counsel of the Lord stands forever, The plans of His heart from generation to generation. Blessed is the nation whose God is the Lord, The people whom He has chosen for His own inheritance. Psalm 33:10-12*

Their counsel was presented, their plan was formulated and their offer was tendered.

Like Pharaoh, God hardened Arafat's heart and he refused the offer!

God did not allow their counsel and their plans to succeed. Just as He said in His Word, "*the Lord nullifies the counsel of the nations*" and "*He frustrates the plans of the peoples.*"

The "*counsel of the Lord stands forever*" and once again, the world is witness to the faithfulness of God despite the unfaithfulness and disobedience of Israeli and American leaders.

WHY THERE WILL BE NO PEACE IN THE MIDDLE EAST

Conflicts are nothing new. There have been many wars fought in the 20th century, and all ended in settlements. So, why should a settlement be impossible in the Middle East?

The Middle East Conflict is unique in that it has three distinct components.

The first is *Physical.*
The second is *Spiritual.*
The third is *"The will of God for Israel in the last days!"*

PHYSICAL CONFLICT

When there is a conflict between nations and peoples, the conflict is usually over physical properties or assets such as land, oil, mineral rights, waterways, etc. These types of conflicts involve tangible things and are by nature, negotiable. Customarily, men sit around a table and come to some form of compromise, which creates the grounds for a settlement. The settlement is a compromise over assets.

The recent so called "peace process" revolved around Israel ceding land to the Palestinians under the assumption that this would bring about peace. Supposedly, the conflict was over how *much* territory Israel would cede to the Palestinians. The issue in the Middle East has no compromise because of the way the Islamic fundamentalists view the conflict over the land of Israel. They do not simply want *more*, they want the whole thing.

The world has been deceived into thinking that if only stubborn Israel would yield, retreat and give up some of their land, peace would suddenly spring forth in the Middle East. By this reasoning, it would appear that the conflict is primarily physical in nature and therefore, negotiable. But the physical component is not the crux of the matter. It goes far deeper than that.

SPIRITUAL CONFLICT

When we move into the realm of "spiritual conflict," those conflicts in which ideological components prevail, there is nothing to negotiate. The basic components of spiritual conflicts simply have no compromise.

The Hamas Charter states that the *entire* land of Palestine is Waqf land, and a "Holy endowment" given to the Arab people by Allah, the god of Islam.

Arafat has said it many times. He does not want peace. He wants all of Israel! Islamic fundamentalists view the land as their holy possession, given to them by their god. Sound familiar? Therefore, according to Islam, there is nothing to negotiate.

Islam declares that all Jews are the enemies of Allah, and therefore have no right to a nation of their own. Islam seeks nothing less than Israel's complete annihilation and nonexistence as a nation and a people. And the nation of Israel cannot negotiate away that which is profoundly not negotiable – their right to exist.

All the United Nations resolutions, peace missions, and condemnations of Israel by the European Union are nothing but a waste of time because in the minds of the Islamic fundamentalists and the Israeli peoples, there is nothing to negotiate.

THE WILL OF GOD FOR ISRAEL IN THE LAST DAYS

The Lord knew that Israel would seek to be like the other nations. They would seek to ignore His command to, *"make no covenant with the inhabitants of the land."*

The Lord prophesied through the prophet Ezekiel this exact situation and its ultimate outcome.

> *"What comes into your mind will not come about, when you say: 'We will be like the nations, like the tribes of the lands, serving wood and stone.' As I live," declares the Lord God, "surely with a mighty hand and with an outstretched arm and <u>with wrath poured out, I shall be king over you.</u> I will bring you out from the peoples and gather you from the lands where you are scattered, with a mighty hand and with an outstretched arm and <u>with wrath poured out;</u> and I will bring you into the wilderness of the peoples, and there I will enter into judgment with you <u>face to face.</u> As I entered into judgment with your fathers in the wilderness of the land of Egypt, so I will enter into judgment with you," declares the Lord God. "<u>I will make you pass under the rod, and I will bring you into the bond of the covenant;</u> and I will purge from you the rebels and those who transgress against Me; I will*

bring them out of the land where they sojourn, but they will not enter the land of Israel. Thus you will know that I am the Lord." Ezekiel 20:32-38

Incredibly, more than 2,500 years ago the Lord prophesied through Ezekiel that the day would come when God would resurrect Israel from the ashes of human history to be a nation once again.

The Lord said, *"What comes into your mind will not come about, when you say, 'We will be like the nations.'"*

The Lord is declaring plainly that *no matter what* the Foreign Ministers, Presidents, Prime Ministers and Kings, the Arab nations, the United Nations, the European Union, and the United States propose and declare regarding Israel, it will all come to nothing!

WHY WILL ALL THEIR PLANS FAIL?

The First "Why"
God said,
"I shall be king over you (Israel)*, not man."*

God is going to have the last word no matter what *men* propose regarding Israel and Jerusalem.

The Second "Why"
God said,
"I will bring you out from the peoples and gather you from the lands where you are scattered, with a mighty hand and with an outstretched arm and with wrath poured out."

God's *purpose* for Israel in the last days is to bring *"all His people back from the lands where He had scattered them!"*

God is true to His word. He is bringing His people back in the midst of war, terror, violence and wrath. All of the nations of the earth will oppose Israel, yet God will prevail and nothing will stand against God's plan for His people in the last days.

The Third "Why"
God said,
"I will bring you into the wilderness of the peoples, and there I will enter into judgment with you face to face."

God is going to bring all His people back to Israel and there He will enter into judgment with them *"face to face."* Talk about terrifying! Meeting the God of Israel face to face where He will enter into judgment with all Israel! Yet God has a plan and a purpose for Israel.

The Fourth "Why"
God said,
"I will make you pass under the rod, and I will bring you into the bond of the covenant."

God is going to make a new covenant with Israel. His *purpose for Israel* is to bring them back into a covenant relationship with Him. His *purpose for Israel* is for them to be His people and for Him to be their God. What an incredible promise!

> *"Behold, days are coming," declares the Lord, "when I will make a new covenant with the house of Israel and with the house of Judah, not like the covenant which I made with their fathers in the day I took them by the hand to bring them out of the land of Egypt, My covenant which they broke, although I was a husband to them," declares the Lord. But this is the covenant which I will make with the house of Israel after those days," declares the Lord, "I will put My law within them and on their heart I will write it; and I will be their God, and they shall be My people. They will not teach again, each man his neighbor and each man his brother, saying, 'Know the Lord,' for they will all know Me, from the least of them to the greatest of them," declares the Lord, "<u>for I will forgive their iniquity, and their sin I will remember no more.</u>" Jeremiah 31:31-34*

All Israel is going to pass under the rod and be brought into the bond of the *"new covenant."* This covenant is going to be different from His first covenant with Israel.

The Fifth "Why"
God said,

"I will put My law within them and on their heart I will write it; and I will be their God, and they shall be My people.

God is not going to write His new covenant on "tablets of stone" *as He did with Moses on Mount Sinai, but this time, God will write His covenant on* "hearts of human flesh."

The Sixth "Why"
God said,

"For they will all know Me, from the least of them to the greatest of them."

All of Israel is going to "know the Lord, from the least of them to the greatest of them!"

What a revelation! All of Israel - every man, woman and child, from every position, walk and station in life, all of Israel - will know the Lord!

The Seventh "Why"
God said,

"For I will forgive their iniquity, and their sin I will remember no more."

By their entering into the new covenant with God, *"godliness"* will replace *"ungodliness."* Before the Lord, Israel will be a *"spotless wife without blemish."* Israel will become a wife purified and clean, and her sins God will *"remember no more."*

The Eighth "Why"
God said,

"I will purge from you the rebels and those who transgress against Me."

Those leaders and people, who like those before them, have said in their hearts, *"Who is the Lord that I should obey Him?"* (Exodus 5:2) and *"The Lord will do no good or evil"* (Zephaniah 1:12) will be judged, purged and removed because they have transgressed against the Lord God of Israel.

The Ninth "Why"
God said,
"Thus you will know that I am the Lord."

In the last days, God will leave no doubt in their hearts and minds that He is the Lord God of Israel. They will have watched Him work wonders among them; they will have been judged by Him face to face; they will have entered into a new covenant with Him and they will stand before Him spotless and clean. All of Israel will *know* that *"I am the Lord."*

CHAPTER 13

THE COMING BATTLE

Jerusalem and the Temple Mount are at the heart and soul of the Middle East issue.

In the days ahead, you will clearly see that the very heart of the controversy in Israel will be the attempt by Arafat, in representing the PLO (Palestinian Liberations Organization), the Arab Muslim nations, the United Nations, the European Union, and even the United States, to force Israel to cede sovereignty and control over part of Jerusalem and the Temple Mount to the Muslim Palestinians and to their god, the god of Islam.

In the name of a false peace the world will demand Israel give that which is holy over to that which is unholy!

Why, as we enter the year 2002, will the coming battle over Jerusalem and the Temple Mount be so fierce?

- The battle will be fierce because Jerusalem is the city where the Messiah will return to earth.

- The battle will be fierce because the East Gate on the Temple Mount is the exact place where the Messiah will return and enter the Temple Mount.

- The battle will be fierce because the Temple Mount is where He will walk into the rebuilt third Temple to sit on His throne to judge and rule the nations!

- The battle will be fierce because it is the exact place where the soles of His feet will stand, where He will rule and reign, and be the eternal God to His chosen people – Israel.

That is why the Temple Mount and Jerusalem are at the very heart and soul of the battle.

Remember that the Middle East conflict has three components: Physical, Spiritual and The Will of God for Israel in the Last Days. The battle in the Middle East is the earthly (or physical) version of the battle that is engaged in the heavenly (spiritual) realm. Allow us to explain further.

The Bible teaches that there is an adversary to God and to the people of God. He is described as a destroyer, a liar and a thief. He opposes the plans and purposes of God and has a spiritual army that works through the minds and hearts of his followers to accomplish his will. He is the enemy of God, His word and His people. His name is Satan, known as the Devil, and all mankind is acquainted with him.

Satan wants to thwart the plans, prophecies and purposes of the God of Israel and control the Temple Mount so his people can worship him there!

Satan believes that if the god of Islam controls East Jerusalem and the Temple Mount, there will never be a third Jewish Temple built, and that the Lord will have nowhere to go when He returns but into the house of Islam, the Al Aksa Mosque.

When we view the battle for Jerusalem and the Temple Mount through God's eyes rather than human eyes, astounding revelation comes forth.

By reading the book of Ezekiel, Chapter 43, we gain true insight into the reason the Temple Mount is at the very heart and soul of the battle for Jerusalem. Satan knows all too well the significance of the Temple Mount. As the enemy of God for untold millennia, Satan also *knows* that the Bible is the word of God. And in it, the Lord declared:

> *And the glory of the LORD came into the house by the way of the gate facing toward the east. He said to me, "Son of man, this is the place of My throne and the place of the soles of My feet, where I will dwell among the sons of Israel forever. This is the law of the house: its entire area on the top of the mountain all around shall be most holy. Behold, this is the law of the house." Ezekiel 43:4, 7, 12*

Please note once again the following important points: Satan knows the significance of the Temple Mount, because the Lord declared it in Ezekiel.

- When the Messiah returns, He will return to Jerusalem.
- The Glory of the Lord will enter Jerusalem as the Messiah enters through the East Gate of the Old City.
- The Messiah will walk onto the Temple Mount.
- His house will occupy the entire area of the Temple Mount.
- The entire top and all around the Temple Mount shall be most holy to God.
- The Messiah will dwell in His house, which is the rebuilt third Jewish Temple located on the Temple Mount.
- The Messiah will dwell among the sons of Israel forever, and He will be their God, and they will be His people.

The battle over the Temple Mount is at the heart and soul of the Middle East conflict as the nations seek to force Israel to divide Jerusalem and give sovereignty over the Temple Mount to the god of Islam.

Scripture has given us clear insight into the true basis of the conflict raging here in Israel. The conflict has never been about peace but rather it is a conflict over God's word, His holy city, His house, His Mount, His people, His covenant and His faithfulness!

Satan wants to replace God and he wants to be worshiped as God. Satan wants to *be* God.

There will be no peace in Israel because Satan is determined to make the Temple Mount the place where his people will worship him and where his house will be established rather than that of the God of Israel's coming Messiah, the redeemer of Israel!

Oh, how we should all rejoice when the Lord gives us spiritual revelation of such things. Biblical insight gives us the ability to see current events in Israel through God's eyes, instead of our human eyes.

KING SOLOMON'S PRAYER OF DEDICATION ASKING THE LORD
TO REMEMBER THE TEMPLE MOUNT AND HIS TEMPLE

"But will God indeed dwell on the earth? Behold, heaven and the highest heaven cannot contain You, how much less this house which I have built! Yet have regard to the prayer of Your servant and to his supplication, O LORD my God, to listen to the cry and to the prayer which Your servant prays before You today; that Your eyes may be open toward this house night and day, toward the place of which You have said, 'My name shall be there,' to listen to the prayer which Your servant shall pray toward this place. Listen to the supplication of Your servant and of Your people Israel, when they pray toward this place; hear in heaven Your dwelling place; hear and forgive."
I Kings 8:27-30

The Lord said that His eyes would be open toward the place of which He has said, "My name shall be there." *And that place is none other than the Temple Mount in Jerusalem!*

GOOD NEWS

After an extensive search of Scripture, I did not find a single verse where the Lord returns and goes into the Al-Aksa Mosque on the Temple Mount and is greeted by Yasser Arafat!

Praise God that when He returns, He will go into the rebuilt third Jewish Temple, where He will rule and reign with a rod of iron for a thousand years!

WOE TO THE NATION'S LEADERS WHO SAY THE GOD OF
ISRAEL WILL DO NO GOOD OR EVIL

It will come about at that time that I will search Jerusalem with lamps, And I will punish the men who are stagnant in spirit, who say in their hearts, "The LORD will not do good or evil!" Zephaniah 1:12

Look around you today. Where are the great Pharaoh's? Where is Hitler? Where is the mighty Soviet Union? Where is Bill Clinton? Where is Ehud Barak? Where is Yitzhak Rabin?

We give praise and glory to the God of Israel! We praise Him for His faithfulness to His word and to His covenant promises even when our leaders are unfaithful!

> *The LORD nullifies the counsel of the nations; He frustrates the plans of the peoples. The counsel of the LORD stands forever, The plans of His heart from generation to generation. Blessed is the nation whose God is the LORD, The people whom He has chosen for His own inheritance. Psalm 33:10-12*

What is taking place in Israel today has absolutely nothing whatever to do with peace or what the politicians and news media call "the peace process."

As the year 2002 continues to unfold, what is taking place in Israel has *everything* to do with only one subject, God's eternal plan for Israel in the last days.

Where Israel is concerned, the Lord is going *"to nullify the counsel of nations,"* and that includes the United Nations, the European Union, the Arab nations, as well as all the other nations.

No matter how many plans or proposals come forth regarding Israel from Presidents, Prime Ministers, Foreign Ministers, Secretaries of State, Kings or Princes, the Lord will frustrate their plans and they will all come to nothing!

Only the Lord's plans for Israel will stand in the last days.

Why is this so? Because the Lord said,

> *"Blessed is the nation whose God is the LORD, The people whom He has chosen for His own inheritance." Psalm 33:12*

He has declared it and He will do it!

CHAPTER 14

POSITION YOURSELVES

The nation of Israel entered the year 2002 at war with the Palestinians. Led by Yasser Arafat, the Palestinians were, and still are determined to drive Israel from the land and possess the entire land of Israel.

WHY IS ISRAEL IN THIS IMPOSSIBLE SITUATION TODAY?

Our leaders do not know nor acknowledge the God of Israel. They continually seek the wisdom of man instead of turning to the God of our fathers to seek His wisdom, His strategy and His deliverance from their enemies. Consequently, Israel is a nation without a Godly strategy to win the war in which it is currently engaged.

Since the beginning of the Intifada in September 2000, Israel has lost hundreds of citizens to Palestinian terrorism, and thousands of innocent men, women and children have been wounded, many seriously. To Israel, this constitutes more dead and wounded than in the entire Six Day War of 1967 against six Arab nations.

Without the Lord's strategy, Israel can never prevail against its enemies. Modern day Israeli governments, past and present, have little understanding of this biblical principle. Few modern Israeli leaders believe that knowing God's strategy is the key to attaining victory in battle.

Israel is a tiny nation, occupying less than 1% of the land surface of the Middle East. The Muslim Arab nations occupy 99% of the entire land surface of the Middle East. But 99% is not enough for the Muslim nations; they demand 100%. So they are seeking Israel's destruction, with the ultimate goal of driving the Jews from the remaining 1% of the land that constitutes the Middle East, into the sea.

The Arab nations have launched seven major wars against Israel in an attempt to remove them from their inheritance, the land of Israel. Currently, Yasser Arafat and the PA are engaged in a bloody war of terrorism against Israel and its citizens. His goal is to force them to give up the land and their capital, Jerusalem.

Until March of 2002, Israel's hands were tied by the United States who, through political pressure, has prevented them from wiping out the Islamic terrorism coming against them. Internally, the situation has been even worse, as the coalition government has been weak and divided.

Israel, for the first time since it became a nation, is facing a situation that most of its citizens believe has no human solution. In the eyes of many citizens, Israel is a nation without hope.

How often we, as people, are like the nation Israel. When the enemy comes against us, we often employ human wisdom and strength to fight, and consequently, we often lose because we have not sought and employed God's strategy in the battle.

During the time of King Jehoshaphat, Israel faced a similar situation in which it was forced to fight for its survival. Present day Israel is a nation at war fighting for its survival, and her current leaders could learn much from reading about King Jehoshaphat.

UNDERSTAND WE ARE ALL ENGAGED IN WARFARE OF ONE KIND OR ANOTHER

All of us are engaged in warfare. No one is exempt. Yet, how few of us really know or understand the weapons of our warfare and how to employ them to effectively fight and win the battle.

King Jehoshaphat was faced with this same challenge. A vast army was marching toward Jerusalem from all sides. What strategy did he choose to employ? Was it human strategy, or was it Godly strategy?

THE ENEMY APPROACHES

In II Chronicles we find Judah, Jerusalem, and King Jehoshaphat in the same situation as Israel finds itself in today.

Now it came about after this that the sons of Moab and
the sons of Ammon, together with some of the Meunites,
came to make war against Jehoshaphat. Then some came
and reported to Jehoshaphat, saying, "A great multitude
is coming against you from beyond the sea, out of Aram
and behold, they are in Hazazon-tamar (that is Engedi).
II Chronicles 20:1-2

If you had been the king and you had received such a report, ask
yourself this question. "What would I have done in this circumstance?"
Would you have assembled the army? Would you have called for the
counsel of all your generals? Would you have called up the reserves?

Israel is a nation today where there is a battle being fought every hour
of every day. It never stops, and the terror just continues to intensify.
To make it worse, the battle in the spiritual realm is just as fierce as it
is in the physical realm.

Each of us face different battles, and they can come in many forms. In
your personal life today you may be battling unemployment, physical
illness, marital problems, fighting addiction to pornography, drugs or
alcohol.

On a national level, Israel is battling with real weapons of warfare,
and with real enemies whose intention is to completely destroy the
nation and the Jewish way of life. What should Israel's strategy be in
this situation? What should your strategy be in the situation you may
be facing as you read this book?

Studying what King Jehoshaphat did in II Chronicles gives us great
insight into understanding the first step Israel must take to win the
battle.

Jehoshaphat was afraid and turned his attention to seek
the LORD, and proclaimed a fast throughout all Judah.
So Judah gathered together to seek help from the LORD;
they even came from all the cities of Judah to seek the
LORD. II Chronicles 20:3-4

108

The first thing we learn in these verses is that Jehoshaphat was afraid. Have you ever been afraid? What did you do to overcome your fear?

Jehoshaphat turned his attention to seek the Lord and proclaimed a fast throughout all Judah.

Ask yourself, if you have really turned your full attention to seek the Lord regarding your personal battles? Turning your attention, to seek the Lord, means getting alone with God and fasting and praying. Fasting is something that most of us do not want to do because it means we must deny our flesh.

Getting alone with God can be a frightening experience, because you cannot lie to God. You must come before Him and bare your heart and soul in spirit and in truth. You must cry out to Him that you recognize that you cannot prevail without His intervention because the enemy is too strong for you.

Getting alone with God is asking Him to fight the battle because our human strength and human strategy is insufficient. It means trusting God completely. It means that if He calls you to go forth and fight the battle, you will trust that He will give you the strategy, that He will go before you and that you will prevail.

Sadly, not a single Israeli leader has turned his attention to seek the Lord and to proclaim a fast throughout Israel. The God of Israel holds the leaders of Israel accountable for their actions, and until one arises who honestly seeks to turn his attention and the attention of the people to seek the Lord, Israel will not prevail in battle.

These verses reveal Jehoshaphat's strategy. He began by seeking the Lord through fasting and prayer. Not only did He seek the Lord in this manner, he called all Israel to do the same. That was the first step in a strategy that would ultimately result in Israel's deliverance from the hand of its enemy and bring glory to the Lord.

Jehoshaphat believed Israel would have to engage in battle against a far superior enemy, but he also understood that if the Lord went before the army of Israel the Lord would receive the glory rather than man, and thus victory was certain.

Jehoshaphat's Prayer

Then Jehoshaphat stood in the assembly of Judah and Jerusalem, in the house of the LORD before the new court, and he said, "O LORD, the God of our fathers, are You not God in the heavens? And are You not ruler over all the kingdoms of the nations? Power and might are in Your hand so that no one can stand against You. Did You not, O our God, drive out the inhabitants of this land before Your people Israel and give it to the descendants of Abraham Your friend forever? They have lived in it, and have built You a sanctuary there for Your name, saying, Should evil come upon us, the sword, or judgment, or pestilence, or famine, we will stand before this house and before You (for Your name is in this house) and cry to You in our distress, and You will hear and deliver us."
II Chronicles 20:5-9

This extraordinary prayer reveals that King Jehoshaphat had a clear understanding of who he was, and who God is. He declared, *"Are you not the God of our fathers, are you not the God in the heavens, and are You not ruler over all the kingdoms and nations?"*

Jehoshaphat was a king, yet he acknowledged that the God of Israel is the ruler over all the kingdoms and nations of the earth.

JEHOSHAPHAT UNDERSTOOD WHERE THE REAL POWER RESIDES

These verses speak volumes about Jehoshaphat's heart, and reveal a clear understanding and recognition of who the God of Israel was in his eyes.

He prayed to God giving recognition that, *"all power and might are in Your hand, so that no one can stand against You!"*

The nation of Israel is suffering horribly today because our leaders do not believe that "all power and might are in the hands of the God of Israel, and that no one can stand against Him."

The Arab nations, the United Nations, the European Union, as well as the United States are all coming against Israel and the God of Israel. The day will come when they too will understand that all power and might are in the hands of the God of Israel, and no nation can stand against Him.

Jehoshaphat understood this fact, and because he understood it, he directed his prayers right to heart of God. He inquired of God on the basis of Scripture and God's promises, fully knowing they are irreversible and stand forever.

The King asked the Lord, *"Did You not, O our God, drive out the inhabitants of this land before Your people Israel and give it to the descendants of Abraham Your friend forever?"*

Why did the king ask God these questions? He asked Him because he knew and understood that *God does not change.*

The God of Israel is the same yesterday, today, and tomorrow.

Jehoshaphat based his prayers upon this truth, and he was exercising his faith based upon what he believed about God. Faith is not blind nor is it dumb. Faith is based on personal experiences in our lives, as well as walking with the Lord and believing that His word and His promises are absolutely true in all circumstances.

Jehoshaphat was putting his faith into action, and he was appealing to God based upon his faith in the promises of God.

Jehoshaphat brings his supplication before the Lord. *"Should evil come upon us, the sword, or judgment, or pestilence, or famine, we will stand before this house and before You (for Your name is in this house) and cry to You in our distress, and You will hear and deliver us."*

Here was a man who understood fully that deliverance and salvation comes from the Lord, and not by the hand or wisdom of man.

How different are the leaders of modern Israel. They believe in the strength and power of the Israeli Defense Force (IDF) and their Air Force. They believe that military power alone can deliver them from the hands of the enemy. The leaders of modern Israel do not understand where the real power lies. Only when the God of Israel goes before the army of Israel, will they see that no one can stand against them.

JEHOSHAPHAT STATES HIS CASE BEFORE THE LORD

"Now behold, the sons of Ammon and Moab and Mount Seir, whom You did not let Israel invade when they came out of the land of Egypt (they turned aside from them and did not destroy them), see how they are rewarding us by coming to drive us out from Your possession which You have given us as an inheritance. "O our God, will You not judge them? For we are powerless before this great multitude who are coming against us; nor do we know what to do, but our eyes are on You."
II Chronicles 20:10-12

King Jehoshaphat was a man who understood God's heart and how to pray effectively about a situation that had no human solution. Jehoshaphat prayed directly to the heart and mind of God, stating exactly what the intentions of the enemy were.

First, he reminds God that Israel did not destroy the sons of Ammon, Moab and Mount Seir when they came out of Egypt and entered the land of Israel.

Israel was innocent of any sin against these enemies that were coming against them now and Jehosphaphat reminds the Lord of this fact.

JEHOSHAPHAT SPEAKS DIRECTLY TO GOD'S HEART

The king drives an arrow directly into the heart of the enemy's plan against Israel. *"See how they are rewarding us by coming to drive us out from Your possession which You have given us as an inheritance."*

Thousands of years later, the enemies of Israel are rewarding Israel's mercy by seeking to drive them out from possessing the land which God gave them as an everlasting inheritance.

Jehoshaphat lays the very heart of the matter before God in prayer. He is saying, "Lord, I believe your word is true! Our enemies do not believe there is a God in Israel, and they do not believe you can defend us.

112

God, they are coming against You, against Your word, against Your people and against your land, against your city Jerusalem that you promised to us as an everlasting inheritance and possession."

Here was a king who understood the power of leading the entire nation in prayer and fasting before the Lord. The king, by his example, was encouraging the entire nation to put their trust in their God, in His word and in His promises.

In times of war, modern Israel is no different from ancient Israel. Its leaders are called upon to believe God's promises are true and put their trust in Him, not in man. Like Israel's leaders, we either believe God's word and His promises, or we don't. With God, there is no middle ground.

GOD DOES NOT CHANGE

"For I, the LORD, do not change; therefore you, O sons of Jacob, are not consumed." Malachi 3:6

Because God is unchangeable, no nation, kingdom, power or principality will ever again succeed in removing Israel from its inheritance. Knowing this fact, believing this fact, and exercising our prayers and faith grounded on this fact enables us all to stand on the word of God, and to experience the faithfulness of the Lord.

Only when Israel's leaders and people turn back to the God of Israel, will they come to know their God, and experience the salvation and deliverance of their God from their enemies.

DON'T LOOK AT THE CIRCUMSTANCES – LOOK TO THE LORD

King Jehoshaphat knew the circumstances facing Israel had no human solution, and that is exactly how the king described Israel's situation to the Lord.

"O our God, will You not judge them? For we are powerless before this great multitude who are coming against us; nor do we know what to do, but our eyes are on You." All Judah was standing before the LORD, with their infants, their wives and their children.
II Chronicles 20: 12-13

Notice Jehoshaphat did not ask the Lord to destroy the enemy. He fully understood that God is the judge of all the earth; that He is righteous and holy. He will judge based upon His righteousness, not man's righteousness.

Jehoshaphat humbled himself before the Lord declaring, *"For we are powerless before this great multitude who are coming against us; nor do we know what to do, but our eyes are on You."*

Today, the situation in Israel is much the same. Israel is strong militarily, but internally its government is divided, making the nation weak and vulnerable. For seven years the leaders of Israel have pursued a policy that is directly opposed to God's will for the nation. They have sought to make a covenant with the inhabitants of the land, to divide the land, to divide Jerusalem and hand it over to a foreign god.

What are the consequences of this policy? First, Israel has experienced bloodshed on an unprecedented scale from the Palestinians. Secondly, the Lord has allowed division in the government and division and fear to enter into the hearts of the people, which has led to a feeling of hopelessness.

It is a fact of biblical history that no nation can be divided against itself and have any hope of defeating its enemies. Only when Israel's leaders turn back to the God of Israel will He remove the division, remove the terror, remove the fear and remove their enemies.

Externally, Israel is surrounded by a multitude of Arab nations that seek her destruction, while division, jealousy, and the absence of faith in their God are tearing the nation apart internally.

Unlike King Jehoshaphat, the eyes of Israel's leaders are focused on the circumstances, the nations, and the wisdom of man rather than giving their attention to and focusing on the Lord God of Israel.

ISRAEL NEEDS A JEHOSHAPHAT

"Oh, God," we pray, "where is the Israeli leader today who will stand before You in prayer and fasting seeking your protection, your wisdom, and your strategy to defeat our enemies?"

"Oh, God," we pray, "where is the Israeli leader today who will call forth an assembly of all Israel to fast, to pray, and to repent before the You?"

ISRAEL IS A NATION WITH NO STRATEGY TO DEFEAT THE ENEMY

Because there is no leader in Israel today with a heart for God like Jehoshaphat, Israel is a nation facing a situation with no feasible solution. There is simply no strategy in Israel today on how to defeat the enemy because the God of Israel is not part of the equation.

Pray that the Lord will have mercy on Israel and bring forth a leader with the heart and the faith of a Jehoshaphat!

GOD ANSWERS JEHOSHAPHAT'S PRAYER

> *Then in the midst of the assembly the Spirit of the LORD came upon Jahaziel the son of Zechariah, the son of Benaiah, the son of Jeiel, the son of Mattaniah, the Levite of the sons of Asaph; and he said, "Listen, all Judah and the inhabitants of Jerusalem and King Jehoshaphat: thus says the LORD to you, 'Do not fear or be dismayed because of this great multitude, for the battle is not yours but God's.'" II Chronicles 20:14-15*

Notice! What does God say to Judah and all the inhabitants of Jerusalem in these verses? *"Do not fear or be dismayed because of this great multitude, for the battle is not yours but God's."*

This one verse contains God's entire strategy for the salvation and the deliverance of Judah and the inhabitants of Jerusalem from the hand of the enemy. There is always victory when we understand fully that the battle is not ours, but the Lords. Pray that the eyes and hearts of Israel's leaders will be opened and turned back to the Lord, so that they will understand this battle is not *theirs*, but the Lord's!

POSITION YOURSELVES – STAND AND SEE THE SALVATION OF THE LORD ON YOUR BEHALF

> *"Tomorrow go down against them. Behold, they will come up by the ascent of Ziz, and you will find them at the end of the valley in front of the wilderness of Jeruel. You need not fight in this battle; station yourselves, stand and see the salvation of the LORD on your behalf, O Judah and Jerusalem. Do not fear or be dismayed; tomorrow go out to face them, for the LORD is with you."*
> *II Chronicles 20:16-17*

Imagine the astonishment of King Jehoshaphat when he heard the Lord say to him, *"You need not fight this battle!"*

Most of us go forward to fight life's battles in our own strength, in our own wisdom and in our pride and arrogance believing that we are greater than God, or that we do not need God to fight our battles. Some even believe that God is *incapable* of fighting our battles. That is exactly why we lose so many of them, and why the enemy is so successful in overcoming and defeating us.

This is precisely why Israel is losing the battle today. They are fighting the battle in their own strength and using human wisdom. That is why the battle is going against them. To prevail, all Israel must do is exactly what Jehoshaphat did! Return to their God!

> *Thus says the LORD of hosts, "Return to Me," declares the LORD of hosts, "that I may return to you," says the LORD of hosts. Zechariah 1:3*

ISRAEL IS DELIVERED BY THE HAND OF GOD FROM THE HANDS OF THEIR ENEMIES

Imagine! The Lord God of Israel commanded the king and all Israel to *"Station yourselves, stand and see the salvation of the Lord on your behalf, O Judah and Jerusalem!"*

Have you ever witnessed *"the salvation of the Lord on your behalf?"* *Israel* did *in this incredible event as recorded in the Bible!*

HAS GOD CHANGED?

Does this same strategy apply to Israel today? God's command to Israel was, *"Position Yourselves!"*

Here He further revealed His strategy to them. He revealed to the king exactly where the enemy was and where to *"position themselves"* for the coming battle.

The Lord then spoke the most incredible words yet! *"You need not fight in this battle!"* How was it possible that Israel could go forth and not have to engage the enemy or fight against this great army, and still prevail?

The answer was revealed in God's prophetic words to the king in 2 Chronicles 20:15: *"....For the battle is not yours but God's".*

Once human strategy is replaced by Godly strategy the enemy is always defeated. Because then, the battle is the Lord's, not ours.

Once Israel turns and stands in God's strategy, in His power and in His might, only then will they finally see and experience the salvation of the Lord on behalf of Israel and Jerusalem.

HOW DO YOU FIGHT THE BATTLE?

Are you facing a battle in your family, in your marriage, in your health, in your finances, with addiction, with lack of faith, or some other seemingly impossible struggle?

When you pray, do you just ask God for deliverance from your problem, or do you pray and seek God's strategy on how to defeat your enemy? There is a *significant* difference.

Knowing and understanding how and what to pray, is far more important than just praying what comes into our minds or praying the same rote prayers everyday.

We all need God's strategy, not our own, to win life's battles. We need to understand and believe that when we turn to God we can also "position ourselves and see the salvation of the Lord on our behalf!"

ISRAEL'S ENEMIES DESTROY THEMSELVES

When the Lord fights our battles the enemy has no chance. We may have to enter the battle, but the outcome is determined before we take our first step forward into the fray.

Israel went forward into the battle, knowing and believing that victory was in the hands of the Lord.

Israel was about to *"See the salvation of the Lord on behalf of Judah and Jerusalem."*

> *When he had consulted with the people, he appointed those who sang to the LORD and those who praised Him in holy attire, as they went out before the army and said, "Give thanks to the LORD, for His lovingkindness is everlasting." When they began singing and praising, the LORD set ambushes against the sons of Ammon, Moab and Mount Seir who had come against Judah; so they were routed. For the sons of Ammon and Moab rose up against the inhabitants of Mount Seir destroying them completely; and when they had finished with the inhabitants of Seir, they helped to destroy one another.*
> *II Chronicles 20:21-23*

WHO WENT BEFORE THE ARMY OF ISRAEL?

Notice it was not cruise missiles, nor the B-52's, nor stealth bombers of today, nor even the chariots that went before the army of ancient Israel, *It was those who sang praises to the Lord and praised Him in Holy attire!*

What did they sing and how did they praise God? They went before the army of Israel singing with trumpets and praising God saying, *"Give thanks to the LORD, for His lovingkindness is everlasting."*

What does this reveal about where the real power and strength lies? It reveals that the greatest power in heaven and on earth is with those who give recognition, praise and glory to God!

Notice what happened immediately when they began to sing and praise the Lord. *When they began singing and praising, the LORD set ambushes against the sons of Ammon, Moab and Mount Seir, who had come against Judah; so they were routed."*

It was the Lord who set the ambush against the sons of Ammon, Moab and Mount Seir, not man! *For the sons of Ammon and Moab rose up against the inhabitants of Mount Seir destroying them completely; and when they had finished with the inhabitants of Seir, they helped to destroy one another."*

It was the Lord, and not man, who caused the enemy to turn against one another and to completely destroy them!

HOW GREAT WAS THE DEVASTATION OF THE ENEMY?

> *"When Judah came to the lookout of the wilderness, they looked toward the multitude, and behold, there were corpses lying on the ground, and no one had escaped." II Chronicles 20:24*

Herein we learn the foundational biblical principle of the story of Jehoshaphat. When the Lord fights our battles the enemy is completely and utterly defeated. Victory comes *by* the Lord, *through* the Lord alone. And to the Lord *alone* belongs all glory and praise for He alone is worthy to receive it.

PART II

CHAPTER 15

THE SWORD OF ISLAM PIERCES THE HEART OF AMERICA

September 11, 2001 was the day that changed forever the life of every American, as the sword of Islam struck at the heart and soul of America herself.

As the smoke rose from the ashes of the Twin Towers, if anyone had any doubts about America being one of the primary targets of the Islamic fundamentalist nations, September 11th should have dispelled any doubt. That fateful morning, we all sat glued to our television sets thinking we were watching a Hollywood action movie. Many of us wept in horror and disbelief as we watched the news that chronicled the terrorists flying jumbo jets into the Twin Towers in New York City, and into the consciousness of America.

And what we were eyewitnesses to that day, as we watched our television sets, was not fantasy or Hollywood special effects, but rather the new reality of the Sword of Islamic fundamentalism.

PATRIOTISM IS REBORN IN AMERICA

In the weeks that followed September 11th, many watched and participated in memorial services held in honor of the thousands of innocent souls who perished in this horrendous attack. From these memorial services two significant trends emerged that touched the heart of every American.

The first significant trend to emerge from the ashes of September 11th was the rebirth of patriotism in America. Flags flew everywhere and people sang "God bless America" every chance they could. Suddenly, Americans were proud to be Americans again.

Americans never thought about their borders. They never thought there was vulnerability there. Nor in their skies above, nor in their cities, let alone in their mailboxes. For the first time in the history of

America, the enemy used a biological weapon against our civilian population. Death could now come in a simple letter in your mailbox, at home or at work, and its name was anthrax.

For a short time, Americans forgot their differences, and remembered in the end they were all bound together by a common heritage, and a common love for America.

GOD AND PRAYER RE-ENTERED THE CONSCIOUSNESS OF AMERICA

The second significant trend to emerge from the ashes of the September 11th attack was a keen awareness among many Americans of how far they had strayed from God. Overnight and throughout the land thousands of people flocked into the nation's churches and synagogues.

> *"Now consider this, you who forget God or I will tear you in pieces, and there will be none to deliver. He who offers a sacrifice of thanksgiving honors me; and to him who orders his way aright I shall show the salvation of God."*
> *Psalm 50:22-23*

America is a nation that has become so prosperous, so affluent and so proud that we forgot that it is not our wealth that protects us, but our God.

Many Americans realized on 9-11 that we are as vulnerable as Israel. We are not immune from the terror stalking the world today. Many were driven to seek God in prayer as we all faced new forms of death and terror from the "Islamic merchants of death."

Suddenly, commercial passenger airplanes that carried many to family gatherings, vacation destinations and business meetings became flying missiles bringing death to thousands of innocent people.

Overnight, God and prayer re-entered the consciousness of America.

AMERICANS BEGAN TO IDENTIFY WITH ISRAELI'S

Nine-eleven caused many Americans to identify with Israel. Americans began to understand that war against terrorism is not just Israel's war, but America's war as well.

Americans began to understand that there are nations and peoples who are actively seeking the destruction of our nation and our way of life. Many with insight began to have a keen awareness that the same people who are seeking to destroy Israel are the same ones who are seeking to destroy America.

Who are the nations conspiring against America? They are the Islamic Muslim nations who all have one thing in common. They are all Islamic fundamentalist nations who worship Allah as their god.

> *My soul is among lions; I must lie among those who breathe forth fire, even the sons of men, whose teeth are spears and arrows and their tongue a sharp sword.*
> *Psalm 57:4*

As Americans watched, the jet propelled "arrows" out of our nation's skies used to "breathe forth fire" from the collapsing towers, many felt like the Psalmist, that indeed our souls were among lions that breathe forth fire, and among men whose teeth are spears and arrows. Surely their tongue is a sharp sword. The sword that came forth against America was the sword of Islam.

Americans were confronted with a new kind of enemy in which innocent civilians were the targets.

Harmless and unsuspecting men, women and children are the preferred targets of the Islamic merchants of death, who specialize in terror, violence and destruction as the weapons of their warfare, and perpetrate all in the name of their god – Allah.

The light began to dawn in many Americans hearts and minds that the Islamic fundamentalist nations are conspiring together with one mind to destroy the United States, just as they are seeking the destruction of Israel.

WHAT DID THE TERRORISTS ALL HAVE IN COMMON?

The nineteen men who participated in flying the jumbo jets into the Twin Towers in New York and into the Pentagon in Washington, D.C. all had one thing in common.

Islam was their religion and Allah was their god!

The nations that sent forth the *"Islamic merchants of death"*, who brought the terror, violence, hatred and war to American soil all have one thing in common.

Islam is their religion and Allah is their god!

The nations and groups attacking Israel on a daily basis are financed, supported, trained and supplied with weapons by those nations who have one thing in common.

Islam is their religion and Allah is their god!

WHY DID ISLAMIC FUNDAMENTALISTS ATTACK AMERICA?

Islamic fundamentalists attacked America because America is the nation that thwarted Saddam Hussein's attempt to take over Kuwait, and then Saudi Arabia. America, "the great Satan" in the eyes of most Muslims, stopped Saddam Hussein from taking control of nearly 70% of the worlds proven oil reserves.

When Iraq invaded Kuwait, America used Saudi Arabia as the land base from which to counter-attack and bring Iraq to its knees. Osama bin Laden declared that it was, and remains, his stated purpose to force America out of Saudi Arabia and out of the Middle East.

His attack on America had nothing to do with Israel – it had everything to do with trying to force the U.S. to leave Saudi Arabia and to eventually bring the entire Middle East under the domination of Islamic fundamentalism.

No other nation but America has the will power combined with the military power to confront the Islamic fundamentalist's nations.

The only nation that is standing in the way of the Islamic conquest of the Middle East and Europe, and eventually the entire the western world is America.

To the mind of the Islamic fundamentalist, America must be destroyed at all costs.

Israel has only one major ally left in the world, and that is America. If America is forced to bow its knee to the god of Islam, then the tiny nation of Israel will stand alone against not only the Islamic fundamentalist nations but also the European Union and the United Nations.

In the mind of the Islamic fundamentalist, when America falls, Israel falls. And make no mistake about it; they are determined for Israel to fall.

CHAPTER 16

AMERICA'S DILEMMA

The Islamic Arab nations possess the vast majority of the world's proven oil reserves, so attempting to pacify them has been the first order of business for every American administration.

Consequently, after the attack of September 11th, the administration sought to build a coalition of Muslim Arab nations who would back America against its impending war against Afghanistan, a Muslim nation.

To accomplish this purpose, the administration, along with England and the European Union, sought to deflect the reality of who really attacked America. Why? The primary reason was to keep the oil flowing at all costs from Saudi Arabia, Iran, Kuwait and the other Middle East nations.

The United States and the other Western nations are totally dependent upon Arab oil to meet their energy demands. The United States alone is responsible for consuming about 20% of Arab oil exports - importing an astounding 52% of its daily oil needs from foreign nations.

All the leaders of the western nations know that the blood that flows through the veins of the western world is OIL!

The second reason that America, England and the European Union sought to pacify the Arab nations is because they have allowed millions of Muslims to enter their countries and become citizens.

If nineteen determined Islamic Muslim terrorists could do this much damage to America, how much more damage could be done by the millions living in America, England and Western Europe if they became part of the plot.

GIVE THE ENEMY A FALSE NAME

Why was the enemy called "terrorism" and not Islamic Fundamentalism?

The enemy had to be called terrorism because the Islamic, Muslim nations have the oil, and because there are literally millions of Muslims living in America, England and Western Europe.

On nine-eleven the Americans, the English, and all of Western Europe awakened to the stark reality that the enemy is *within* as well as *without*.

Because of the oil, and because the enemy was within, the nations cloaked themselves in deception, believing it would protect them from the scourge to come.

> *Because you have said, "We have made a covenant with death, and with Shell we have made a pact. The overwhelming scourge will not reach us when it passes by; for we have made falsehood our refuge and we have concealed ourselves with deception." Isaiah 28:15*

All nations perpetrated the great deception that "terrorism" was America's enemy, not Islamic Fundamentalism. And so they named her.

WHERE DID MOST OF THE MEN WHO COMMITED THESE HORRENDOUS TERRORIST ATTACKS COME FROM?

But, where did the majority of the men who committed these incredibly evil acts against America come from?

After months of investigation, the Interior Minister Prince Nayef of Saudi Arabia told the Associated Press on February 7, 2002 that Saudi leaders were shocked to learn that *15 of the 19 hijackers were from Saudi Arabia!*

How could the Saudi Interior Minister be shocked? The well-known Islamic Fundamentalist, Osama bin Laden, millionaire financier, trainer and exporter of terrorism worldwide, is *from* Saudi Arabia!

FOLLOWING THE MONEY TRAIL

It costs hundreds of millions of dollars to finance and fund an organization like Al Qaida. It took millions to buy weapons and to establish terrorist training camps. It took more millions to train and indoctrinate terrorists as well as develop anthrax and other chemical and biological agents as weapons of war. In the end, it took more millions to deploy Al Qaida agents throughout the western world and in America.

Once in America, it took hundreds of thousands of dollars to fund their living costs, and to pay for the attackers to enter flying schools where they were trained to fly, and would later use that knowledge to fly jumbo jets into the Twin Towers and the Pentagon!

WHERE DID AL QAIDA FUNDING COME FROM?

The American administration, England and the European Union, immediately moved to cut off the flow of funds to Al Qaida originating in America and Western Europe. However, the amounts confiscated were only a small portion of the vast river of funds flowing through the veins of this terrorist organization.

So where did the vast sum of money come from to fund Al Qaida? Remember, we are not speaking here about millions of dollars, but hundreds of millions of dollars, and possibly billions.

Look at the countries from which these terrorists came! Look at the Islamic fundamentalist nations who ferment hatred for America and Israel and you will find the source of the money.

Yet, no one dares to state the truth because OIL is more important than truth!

WHAT IS TERRORISM?

Sadly, Americans woke up one morning and, innocence gone began to understand that the same people who committed "terrorist attacks" against America on September the 11th were the same ones committing "terrorist acts" against Israel. The same people, from some of the same nations, who worship the same god, are also the ones who are financing, training and supplying the weapons that are killing and wounding Israeli's on a daily basis.

During 2001 and 2002, when a suicide bomber would blow himself up in Jerusalem or Tel Aviv, the U.S. State Department, the E.U., and the English Foreign Office would condemn the attack. Not surprisingly though, when Israel would respond in self-defense, the same U.S. State Department, the European Union and the English Foreign Office would arise like lions and condemn Israel for using "excessive force."

Incomprehensibly, the U.S. State Department, the European Union and the British Foreign Office were all telling the world that "terrorism in America" is different from "terrorism in Israel."

They put forth the incredible lie to the world that Palestinians who murder innocent men, women, and children in *Israel* are not terrorists they are "freedom fighters."

According to the U.S. Department of State, the acts of Islamic militants who have killed and wounded thousands of innocent men, women and children in America are acts of terrorism. However, when the very same Islamic fundamentalists kill and wound thousands of innocent Israeli and Arabic men, women and children in Israel, it is *not* terrorism.

THE U.S. STATE DEPARTMENT'S DOUBLE STANDARD

In early 2002, the State Department announced a new policy regarding listing the names of Palestinian terrorists who had injured or murdered Americans. Incredibly, they have reversed this policy now and decided *not* to reveal the names of Palestinian Arab terrorists who have murdered or injured American citizens.

In a recently released report to Congress on United States efforts to capture such terrorists, the State Department notes that the names of the wanted Arab terrorists will not be listed. A spokesman explained that this was done in order to "not glorify them."

However, the Zionist Organization of America notes that the State Department has no problem listing the names of terrorists who are not Palestinian Arabs.

President Morton A. Klein declared:

"This is the latest in a series of actions by the State Department which force us to question why it is not doing everything it can to capture Palestinian Arab killers of Americans? Does the State Department really expect the American public to believe that publishing photos of Fattah and Hamas terrorists who kill Americans would 'glorify' them, while somehow the State Department's own publication of the photos of terrorists from Al Qaida, Hezbullah, Egyptian Islamic Jihad, and Libya does not glorify those terrorists?"

Klein added, "This incredible double standard is part of the State Department's appeasement policy of bending over backwards to avoid embarrassing Yasser Arafat. The State Department knows that publicly mentioning the names of the suspects in these cases would mean drawing attention to the fact that the suspects include two long-time confidantes of Arafat; three officials of Arafat's Palestinian Authority; three members of Arafat's Force 17 presidential guard; and five members of Arafat's security forces."

Sadly, all Israel knows that in the eyes of the U.S. State Department, the government of England, the European Union and the combined Arab Nations, Palestinians murdering, wounding and terrorizing innocent men, women and children in Israel, their own included, is not considered "terrorism."

Sadly also, all Israel knows that in America when innocent people are murdered or injured by terrorists, somehow the colors change and in Red, White and Blue the act becomes "terrorism."

A new definition of *"terrorism"* has emerged from our U.S. State Department, from the English government, and the European Union.

"Terrorism is terrorism only when it is committed against Americans, English or Europeans."

If the *same* acts of violence and terror are committed against Israeli's by the *same* people who worship the *same* god of Islam, then is it not the same? Is it not "terrorism?"

The Jewish blood of innocent men, women and children, spilled in crowded restaurants and on city buses, at Passover celebrations and in pizza parlors, asks America, England and Europe, "What makes this so different?"

In the eyes of the U.S. Department of State, the British, and the E.U., "Oil is far more important than Jewish blood!"

CHAPTER 17

FINANCING THE PALESTINIAN AUTHORITY

The primary source of funds to the Palestinian Authority and Yasser Arafat's terrorist organization comes from the European Union and the Arab nations.

On Oct. 22, 2001, when Israeli forces burst into the Ramallah headquarters of Arafat's presidential guard known as Force 17, they found an extraordinary set of documents containing proof that the Palestinian Authority (PA) leader, Yasser Arafat, was paying the entire body of Tanzim-Fatah terrorists out of His own "presidential" budget. The figures were there in black and white for the entire world to see.

Every one of the 10,000 Tanzim activists on Arafat's payroll was receiving 875 New Israeli Shekels, and *has* been ever since Arafat launched his armed confrontation in September 2000. The captured documents included Arafat's signed directive, issued three weeks before the outbreak of the Intifada, to pay $22,000 to each of the leading Fatah terror masters into their personal accounts, to defray the costs of creating the terror body named the Tanzim.

The documents showed exactly how Arafat's office transfers the Tanzim payroll to the Ramallah offices of Force 17, whose paymasters distributed the wage packets. In addition to these documents found in September 2000, the Jerusalem Post reports as late as May 14, 2002 that the Palestinian Authority Chairman Yasser Arafat's direct involvement in personally approving funding for terrorist attacks has been reconfirmed by details released by the Shin Bet security agency from its interrogation of senior Fatah Tanzim leader Nasser Abu Hamid.

A simple reckoning shows that in the first fourteen months of the Intifada, the European taxpayer has been contributing - unknowingly but regularly - around $2,190,000 per month to keep the Palestinian terrorist Tanzim militia afloat, a total of $31 million since Arafat began his attack to destroy Israel. The Arab nations, during this period, contributed an astounding $40 million a month to finance Palestinian terror.

Interestingly, in early February of 2002, the Middle East news source, "Debka File" published the following report:

> "Just over three weeks ago, Palestinian Authority paymasters, about to hand out January wage packets to civilian and security personnel, were taken aback to find that the $50 million earmarked for the purpose had gone missing. At a loss, they asked their bosses what to do and were told there was nothing for it but to take the problem to Yasser Arafat.
>
> However, in the top man's presence, no one said a word. Every one of those staffers knew exactly who had taken the money and on what it was spent. Arafat's latest Fatah-Tanzim terror cycle, already referred to by insiders as the "Palestinian Tet Offensive."
>
> "So what's the problem," asked Arafat. "The missing January payroll," he was told. For the sake of appearances, the Palestinian leader bawled everyone out, before announcing he would find the money.
>
> From where? The Europeans, of course!
>
> After a couple of telephone calls from Ramallah to the European Union foreign affairs executive, Javier Solana - $30 million was forthcoming to rescue the January payroll.
>
> When Solana arrived in the region on Monday, February 25, some of his Israeli contacts filled him in on the destination of the missing payroll funds. They indicated that if the episode came out, the European Union could hardly avoid being accused of using European tax revenues to fund Palestinian terror. This notion irked even Solana.

So on Monday, when he called on Arafat in his Ramallah office, he demanded that the Al Aqsa Martyrs' Brigades – a wing of Arafat's Fatah – be disbanded forthwith. He did not go so far as to mention the Fatah-Tanzim militia."

Because of Arab oil, the European Union has become a proxy for the Arab nations, acting as one of the primary paymasters to Yasser Arafat and his terrorist organization!

So America's allies, the European Union are one of the primary sources of financing for the Palestinian Authority, and are marching in lock step with the Arab nations to destroy the nation of Israel.

SAUDI MONEY

Saudi Arabia has launched a strong publicity campaign in the United States to try and repair its image as a *"moderate Arab nation."* Yet, the facts in the matter are quite contrary to the half-truths and lies being put forth in their current publicity campaign.

On May 6, 2002, there was a press conference held at the Israeli Embassy in Washington, D.C. The Minister of Education, Limor Livnat, disclosed documents at that press conference showing that Saudi Arabia funneled $135 million over the last 16 months to Hamas and to the families of dead terrorists.

This information is now in the public domain, and there are hopes that the public, the media and members of Congress will now begin to ask how the United States, in its war on terror, can cozy up to a Saudi regime that in the words of the Military Intelligence report state, *"transferred large sums of money in a systematic and ongoing manner to families of suicide terrorists, to the Hamas organization, (listed on the US list of terrorist organizations), and to individuals and entities identified with Hamas."*

The Saudi government speaks one way to the western press, while their newspapers, radio and television daily pour forth hate and venom toward Israel and America.

A few samples from the Saudi press tell the story quite graphically:

> "Life stopped in 'Israel' yesterday for two minutes [Holocaust Memorial Day siren] while the warning siren whistled all over the occupied territories of Palestine, in memory of the 6 million Jews, about whom 'Israel' lies, saying that they were killed in the Nazi crematoriums during the World War II." (Article, Ar-Riyadh, April 10, 2002)

> "I need to tell the president of the United States, 'Mr. President, for God's sake, don't talk like an evil man who cannot escape from an evil choice. It is better to be dumb than to speak like an evil accomplice who financed Zionist warlords and launched an evil crusade against Muslims everywhere...'" "The bitter truth, of course, is that the Bush White House is not interested in understanding the realities of history. White House involvement is driven simply by the domestic political need to keep Zionist opinion sweet back home, in the face of this year's mid-term elections. Therefore, any American voting the Republican ticket is effectively marking his voting with Palestinian blood." (Editorial, Arab News, April 18, 2002)

ARAFAT AND IRANIAN ALLIANCE

On March 24, 2002, the New York Times reported that intelligence officials had concluded that Yasser Arafat has forged a new alliance with Iran that involves Iranian shipments of heavy weapons and millions of dollars to Palestinian groups that are waging guerrilla warfare against Israel.

Questions about Iran's relationship with the Palestinians came into public view early in 2002, when Israel seized a ship, the Karin-A, carrying 50 tons of Iranian-supplied arms. Included in this shipment were large numbers of antitank weapons that could have neutralized one of Israel's main military advantages over the Palestinians along with rockets that could be used in attacks against most of Israel's cities and population centers.

DOCUMENTS PROVE ARAFAT'S PALISTINIAN AUTHORITY SPONSORED TERRORISM

Original documents seized by IDF forces in Arafat's Ramallah compound in early April of 2002, reveal a direct link between official elements of the Palestinian Authority and the terrorist organization known as the Al-Aqsa Brigades. Al-Aqsa, a branch of Arafat's Fatah organization, has perpetrated numerous terror attacks over the past eighteen months, killing scores of Israelis.

One document, for example, is a correspondence between Al-Aqsa officials and Fuad Shubaki, Arafat's chief finance officer and the man who organized the Karin-A arms-smuggling ship.

The document records a request by Al-Aqsa that Shubaki fund bombs to be used in suicide bombing attacks against Israelis. The document is very specific: "*The cost of making one explosive charge is at least 700 shekels [and] each week we require five to nine bombs for cells operating in various regions.*" The document also shows that Shubaki transferred monthly salaries to Al-Aqsa members for their terrorist activities.

THE EUROPEAN UNION SUPPORTS TERROR

It is interesting to note what the European Union did after Israel was forced to enter the Palestinian cities and uncover irrefutable proof that E.U. funds were being used to finance terrorist attacks on Israel.

The E.U. counsel voted $43 million in aid to the Palestinians to ostensibly rebuild their infrastructure. The E.U. has knowingly funded the Palestinian Authority terrorist operations, knowing full well that a large part of the funds go to pay for suicide attacks on innocent Israeli's, to buy arms, and to perpetuate the war against Israel.

At the same meeting when the E.U. counsel voted the $43 million in aid to the Palestinian Authority, Germany and England independently imposed an arms embargo against Israel. No such arms embargo was imposed on the Palestinian Authority.

ARAFAT IS A TERRORIST

The Jerusalem Post, on April 6, 2002, based upon the questioning of senior Fatah terrorist in Israeli custody, Marwan Barghouti, reported the following:

> "The fact that Yasser Arafat personally approved terrorist funding for Fatah has now become 'unequivocally clear', announced the Israeli Prime Minister's office.

Israeli investigators have learned that Fatah head Marwan Barghouti, who maintained direct communications with Arafat, transferred money to Fatah operatives specifically for attacks targeting and killing many Israeli civilians.

> *'These disclosures render absurd the public and international debate over whether Arafat is 'doing everything possible to prevent terrorism,'*

Prime Minister Sharon's Office stated, explaining that it is now clear that he indeed did 'everything possible' to promote, not prevent, terrorism.

Barghouti, who admitted to directing terrorist attacks that resulted in the killing and injuring of scores of Israeli civilians, described in detail the transfer of funds to the terrorist operatives. He was responsible for providing the funding for weapons acquisition and armed operations, and said that every terrorist request for funds was accompanied by a written requisition.

Barghouti would add his recommendation and signature, and then relay the request to PA Chairman Arafat. Barghouti stressed that every expense, no matter how small, required Arafat's personal approval. The funds were then transferred to the operatives according to the instructions of Hakem Bil'awi, the Secretary of the Fatah Central Committee.

Nasser Aweis, head of the Fatah infrastructure in Samaria, was responsible for the recruiting, arming and handling of terrorist cells. He confirmed that he and other Tanzim terrorist operatives under his command received funding directly approved by Yasser Arafat. Aweis admitted to having been behind numerous terrorist bombings and shootings in Israel, including the murder of six Bat Mitzvah celebrants in Hadera, as well as several shooting attacks in Jerusalem and elsewhere that killed eight Israelis.

Nasser Abu Hamid, a commander and founder of the Al Aqsa Martyrs Brigades and who was also arrested during Operation Defensive Shield, revealed during questioning that he and his men received funding and weapons from Marwan Barghouti, through the latter's aide, Ahmed Barghouti. Abu Hamid stated that Marwan knew the details of every operation carried out by himself and his men, and he was involved in the decision regarding the procurement of weapons for the terrorist cells, and even provided the payment approval for these weapons. Abu Hamid and his men were responsible for numerous shooting attacks, explosive charges and suicide bombings, resulting in the deaths of at least six Israelis - including the Kahane couple.

He also revealed that his men received the explosive devices needed for their terrorist operations from Arafat's Force 17 Presidential Guard weapons depots, and that Force 17 members would regularly assemble explosive devices and give them to Fatah terrorists.

WHY IS THERE NO PEACE IN THE MIDDLE EAST?

The Psalmist, Asaph, wrote the answer to this question over 3,000 years ago in the book of Psalms. The Spirit of God came upon him and he wrote of the time in the future when Israel would once again become a nation, and the Arab nations would covenant together to destroy Israel and people of God.

Over 3,000 years ago God revealed and recorded the plan of the Arab nations to destroy Israel in Psalm 83.

> *O GOD, do not remain quiet; Do not be silent and, O God, do not be still. For behold, Your enemies make an uproar, And those who hate You have exalted themselves. They make shrewd plans against Your people, And conspire together against Your treasured ones. They have said, "Come, and let us wipe them out as a nation, That the name of Israel be remembered no more." For they have conspired together with one mind; Against You they make*

a covenant: The tents of Edom and the Ishmaelites, Moab and the Hagrites; Gebal and Ammon and Amalek, Philistia with the inhabitants of Tyre; Assyria also has joined with them; They have become a help to the children of Lot. Psalm 83:1-8

It is interesting to note that in this Psalm the enemies of God have exalted themselves against Him. Today, those who hate the God of Israel are making an uproar among the nations.

Where is this uproar? The uproar is in Israel, in the Sudan, in many countries in the Far East, in many of the European countries and on September 11th the uproar exploded in New York City and Washington, D.C.

What do these verses reveal about the plan of the nations who hate the God of Israel? They have made *shrewd plans* and *conspired together against His treasured ones* – Israel! What are their plans and their purpose?

They have all said, "Come, and let us wipe them out as a nation, that the name of Israel will be remembered no more!"

The reason there is no peace in the Middle East is that the issue is not about peace, and never has been. It is not about creating a Palestinian State, nor is it about Israel ceding land for peace.

The reason there is no peace in the Middle East is because the purpose of Arafat, the Arab Nations, and now the European Union and the United Nations as well, is revealed in this one verse of Psalm 83.

They have said, "Come, and let us wipe them out as a nation, that the name of Israel will be remembered no more!"

In this Psalm written thousands of years ago, the Lord prophesied through the Psalmist, Asaph, that in the last days Israel would become a nation, and that the Arab nations would lead a coalition to destroy the nation that God had resurrected – the nation of Israel. And though it was written thousands of years ago, it reads like today's headlines.

Interestingly, these nations believe they have made a covenant against the Jews and the nation of Israel, when in reality they have made a covenant against the God of Israel. Human history is littered with the ashes of the nations who made a covenant against the God of Israel.

The Arab nations, the United Nations and the European Nations are not exempt from God's judgment.

God does not change!

Imagine! A Psalm written more than 3,000 years ago prophesies *exactly* who would make this covenant against the God of Israel and His treasured ones.

The Arab nations are the ones identified and described in the Psalm, and they are the *very* ones who are leading the coalition of nations seeking Israel's destruction.

There is no peace in the Middle East because the issue is not about peace, or exchanging land for peace.

There is no peace in the Middle East because the Palestinian Authority and the Arab nations don't want peace – they want the destruction of Israel.

Yasser Arafat has declared it a thousand times in Arabic saying, "he does not want peace, he wants all of Israel!"

Because America has taken a stand with the God of Israel and for His treasured ones, Israel, the Arab nations, along with the Palestinian Authority, have conspired with one mind together to destroy America as well. And September 11th 2001, was positive proof.

CHAPTER 18

JERUSALEM - A CUP OF REELING

During the first week of March 2002, the United Nations Security Council convened and voted unanimously for the creation of a Palestinian State to be carved out of the land of Israel.

A Palestinian Muslim state out of the very land God promised to Israel by everlasting covenant!

The United States for the first time in its history voted in favor of this resolution!

Sadly, the United States had given way to the pressures and ploys of the Arab nations, the European Union and the United Nations in calling for a division of Israel and Jerusalem in order to create a Palestinian Muslim nation in the midst of the land of Israel.

Dividing East and West Berlin, North and South Korea, and India and Pakistan has not worked, so what on earth could possibly lead all the nations to believe it will work by dividing Israel and Jerusalem?

What does the Lord say to the nations who seek to remove His people from their inheritance, divide their land and divide Jerusalem?

> *"I will gather all the nations And bring them down to the valley of Jehoshaphat. Then I will enter into judgment with them there On behalf of My people and My inheritance, Israel, Whom they have scattered among the nations; And they have divided up My land." Joel 3:2*

The Lord declared thousands of years ago that the day would come in human history when all the nations would come against Jerusalem and Judah (Israel).

> *"Behold, I am going to make Jerusalem a cup that causes reeling to all the peoples around; and when the siege is against Jerusalem, it will also be against Judah. It will come about in that day that I will make Jerusalem a heavy stone for all the peoples; all who lift it will be severely injured. And all the nations of the earth will be gathered against it." Zechariah 12:2-3*

During the first week of April 2002, this prophecy began to be fulfilled as *all* the nations of the world, including the United States, began their siege against Jerusalem and Judah.

Just as the Word of the Lord declared it would take place, in April of 2002, it did. The day before the U.S. Secretary of State Colin Powell's arrival in Israel on his "peace mission," there was a news conference aired on CNN (Cable News Network).

Assembled together before the CNN television cameras were the representatives of the nations of the world. Standing on the platform together were Kofi Annan, Secretary General of the United Nations, Colin Powell, Secretary of State from the United States, Javier Salinas the leader of the European Union, and the Foreign Minister of the Soviet Union.

When it came time for Colin Powell to speak, he said,

> "We all stand here today united together to give our time, our efforts, and our money to achieve one goal – the creation of a Palestinian State through the restoration of the Palestinian Authority with Yasser Arafat as its leader!"

Incredibly, just as the word of God prophesied, all the nations of the world gathered together to resurrect and establish the arch terrorist Yasser Arafat as the leader of a new Muslim nation carved out of the land promised by God to Israel as an everlasting possession.

WHAT IS THE CUP THAT CAUSES REELING?

For thus the LORD, the God of Israel says to me, "Take this cup of the wine of wrath from My hand and cause all the nations to whom I send you to drink it. They will drink and stagger and go mad because of the sword that I will send among them." Jeremiah 25:15-16

All the leaders of the world's nations, the European Union, the Arab nations, and the United Nations, gather together and proclaim:

"We will not drink of this cup! We are great and powerful! Who can resist our will? We possess the oil, the economic power, the financial resources, the military might and the political power to force our will upon Israel!"

The leaders of the nations gather together and ask themselves: "How can Israel, a nation of only six million people resist the will of the United Nations comprising some six billion people?"

The leaders of the nations gather together and declare: *"We will not drink and stagger and go mad because of the sword the Lord will send among us!"*

The leaders of the nations gather together and say: *"We will cause Israel to drink and to stagger and go mad because the sword of the Arabs is among them!"*

The leaders of the nations gather together and announce: *"We will not drink this cup, we shall make Israel drink this cup!"*

This week the leaders of the all the world's nations declared through the Security Council resolution: *"We will force Israel to divide the land and accept the creation of a Palestinian nation in their midst. We will force them to divide Jerusalem and to create a capital for a Palestinian Muslim nation!"*

Yet, what does the Lord declare about the plans of Presidents, Prime Ministers, Foreign Ministers, Kings and Princes of these nations?

The LORD nullifies the counsel of the nations; He frustrates the plans of the peoples. The counsel of the LORD stands forever, The plans of His heart from generation to generation. Psalm 33:10-11

No matter *what* the Security Council of the United Nations declares: *"The counsel of the Lord will stand forever."*

Though the nations declare, *"We will not drink of this cup!"* the Lord declares, *"You shall surely drink!"*

What is this cup that the nations shall drink, who say, "We will not drink of this cup?"

"You shall say to them, (the nations), Thus says the LORD of hosts, the God of Israel, 'Drink, be drunk, vomit, fall and rise no more because of the sword which I will send among you.' And it will be, if they refuse to take the cup from your hand to drink, then you will say to them, 'Thus says the LORD of hosts: 'You shall surely drink! For behold, I am beginning to work calamity in this city, (Jerusalem), which is called by My name, and <u>shall you be completely free from punishment?</u> You will not be free from punishment; for I am summoning a sword against all the inhabitants of the earth,' declares the LORD of hosts." Jeremiah 25:27-29

The Lord God of Israel declares to all the nations who seek to divide Jerusalem and Judah, *"You shall surely drink of my cup of reeling!"*

What will be in this cup that the Lord of hosts, the God of Israel will cause the nations to drink?

It is a sword, which will be sent among the nations. The cup will be filled with deception and poison, it will cause the nations to be drunk, to vomit, and to fall down and rise no more.

The Lord asks the nations who come against Judah and Jerusalem, *"Shall you be completely free from punishment?"*

143

Then the Lord prophesies to the nations, *"You will not be free from punishment; for I am summoning a sword against all the inhabitants of the earth!"*

While the word, sword, in the Bible is often known as the "Word" of God, here in this particular instance, in this author's opinion it is the sword of Islam. It is the very sword with which the nations of the world have joined forces to lift Jerusalem from its rightful place. And this sword that the nations have used against Israel will be turned against them. It will pierce the nations, it will cut them to pieces, and they will fall and rise no more.

God is prophesying to the nations saying, *"All of the nations who seek to lift the heavy stone of Jerusalem from its rightful place will be severely injured!"*

God is not mocked, nor will His word be changed!

God is the same yesterday, today, and tomorrow. He declared this in the Old Testament, as well as in the New Testament.

> *"For I, the LORD, do not change; therefore you, O sons of Jacob, are not consumed." Malachi 3:6*

> *Jesus Christ is the same yesterday and today and forever. Hebrews 13:8*

All of the nations who are actively seeking the destruction of Israel and to force her *"to drink from the cup of reeling,"* will soon learn that the God of Israel will have the last word.

> *Therefore, please hear this, you afflicted, Who are drunk, but not with wine: Thus says your Lord, the LORD, even your God Who contends for His people, "Behold, I have taken out of your hand the cup of reeling, The chalice of My anger; You will never drink it again. I will put it into the hand of your tormentors, Who have said to you, 'Lie down that we may walk over you.' You have even made your back like the ground and like the street for those who walk over it." Isaiah 51:21-23*

The Lord God of Israel is about to contend for His people. The Lord God of Israel declares in these verses; *"Israel will never drink of this cup again!"*

The Lord God of Israel has a message for the EU, the United Nations, and the Arab nations, and the United States if they join together to divide Jerusalem. The message is embodied in these verses: The Lord God of Israel says to them, *"I will put it (the cup of reeling) into the hand of your tormentors, who have said to you, 'Lie down that we may walk over you.' You have even made your back like the ground and like the street for those who walk over it."*

What the nations of the world do not understand is that the land of Israel, the Jews, and Jerusalem belong to God and to not the nations!

Whoever touches Israel touches the heart of God, the covenants of God, and the apple of God's eye!

The leaders of all the nations should remember and consider strongly what the God of Israel declared to Abraham regarding how they treat his descendants – Israel and the Jews.

> *"And I will bless those who bless you, and the one who curses you I will curse. And in you all the families of the earth will be blessed."* Genesis 12:3

WHY HAS GOD BLESSED AMERICA?

Very few people understand that one of the primary reasons for America's incredible blessings during the past 226 years stems from what the Lord declared to Abraham regarding the nations and people who bless His descendants - the Jewish people.

> *And God said; "I will bless those who bless you, and curse those who curse you."* Genesis 12:3

All nations of the earth who have blessed Israel have been, are being and will continue to be blessed by God. God has promised through His word and through His covenant given to Abraham, Isaac, and Israel (Jacob) in accordance with the written prophecies of the Holy Scriptures, that this would be so.

Americans should understand clearly that the actions of their nation as a whole to bless Israel and the Jewish people are one of the primary reasons why we have been blessed as a nation. Up until this day, Americans have obeyed God's word and prophecy regarding blessing Israel and the Jews, and consequently God's blessings have flowed onto and throughout our nation and our people.

Simply put, God has blessed America because His Word said He would bless those who bless His people!

America, from its inception as a nation, has "blessed the Jews in their midst." In 1948, when the day came for the United Nations to vote to establish the nation of Israel, America voted in favor of the creation of the state of Israel. When Israel was attacked in five major wars by her Arab neighbors, America has always chosen to stand with Israel!

Many Americans fail to make this connection, because they do not know or believe the word of God regarding Israel.

Human history is a testimony to the truth of God's word regarding those who have chosen to bless His people.

Human history is also littered with the ashes of the nations who cursed, persecuted and sought to destroy the Jewish people.

EVERY NATION MUST MAKE A CHOICE - EITHER THEY ARE FOR GOD'S PEOPLE OR THEY ARE AGAINST THEM

In the years ahead, Americans will have to decide whether to continue to stand with or to turn against Israel. The pressure of world events has already begun to bring our government and our people to the point where they must make this all-important decision.

Either Americans will choose to turn away from Israel and follow the other nations of the world, or they will choose to follow God's word, stand with Israel and continue to receive God's blessings. America must choose, and her very life depends on the decision she makes.

The blessings of God always follow obedience to His commands.

Incredibly, many people say they cannot find where America is mentioned or spoken of in the Bible.

America is a nation, and the nations are spoken of in both the Old and New Testaments and mentioned 485 times in 461 verses of The New American Standard Bible.

The verses previously noted in Zechariah 12:2-3 prophesy to the nations of which America is foremost. America is in mortal danger if her leaders turn against Israel.

The President of the United States has stated on numerous occasions that he favors the creation of a Palestinian state carved out of the land promised to Israel as an everlasting possession by God.

THE LORD INTERVENES

In late June of 2002, President George W. Bush was set to make a dramatic announcement regarding America's support for the establishment of a Palestinian State when the Lord intervened.

The day before the announcement was to be made, June 23rd, an Al-Aqsa Brigade Palestinian suicide bomber set off a bomb inside the Egged bus #32, killing 19 Israeli's, and wounding upward to 40 innocent men, women, and children. The President postponed his speech, and evidently changed its entire context.

What caused him to change the context of his speech? No doubt it was the incontrovertible evidence that Arafat had paid the Al-Aqsa Brigade $20,000 to carry out the attack against the Egged bus. The Al-Aqsa Brigade is a front for Fatah, the main faction of the PLO, which is directly under the control of Arafat.

The light had finally dawned in America that no responsible person can speak of suicide bombings without recognizing that they are not individual acts of desperation, but part of a deliberate political campaign on the part of the Palestinian Authority and Yasser Arafat to consciously foster and develop in Palestinian classrooms, in places of worship and through the controlled PA media a generation that "glorifies murdering innocent Israel's."

Sadly, it is also a well-known fact that families of these "terrorists," are most generously rewarded for their children's acts of becoming "Islamic merchants of death" by Saudi Arabia and Iraq, which pays each family of a "successful" suicide attacker $25,000.

In the face of opposition from the U.S. State Department, and the European Union, the President declared publicly that Arafat was a supporter of terrorism, and he called for a new and different Palestinian leadership, so that a Palestinian state can be born.

Although the President called for the removal of Arafat, he called for the establishment of a Palestinian State at a time in the future, on the land promised to Israel by God as an everlasting possession. Sadly, he has adopted the "plan of the nations," rather than the "plan of God" as a solution to the problems in the Middle East. His plan and the plan of the nations to divide Israel and Jerusalem will never prevail because of the word of the God.

> *"It is definitely because they have misled My people by saying, 'Peace!' when there is no peace. And when anyone builds a wall, behold, they plaster it over with whitewash; so tell those who plaster it over with whitewash, that it will fall. A flooding rain will come, and you, O hailstones, will fall; and a violent wind will break out. So I will tear down the wall which you plastered over with whitewash and bring it down to the ground, so that its foundation is laid bare; and when it falls, you will be consumed in its midst. And you will know that I am the LORD. Thus I will spend My wrath on the wall and on those who have plastered it over with whitewash; and I will say to you, 'The wall is gone and its plasterers are gone, along with the prophets of Israel who prophesy to Jerusalem, and who see visions of peace for her when there is no peace,' declares the Lord GOD." Ezekiel 13:10-11, 14-16*

All the nations who seek to lead Israel into a so called "peace agreement," saying there will be peace when there is no peace will fall. Those who seek to whitewash and plaster a framework of peace that divides the land and divides Jerusalem will be consumed. Why will they be consumed?

 Because the Lord will pour out His wrath on the wall, the so called "peace agreement," so its foundation will be laid bare, and when the wall is gone so will its plasterers disappear, along with the prophets of Israel who see visions of peace in Jerusalem when there is no peace. When this takes place all the nations will know and understand that it is the Lord of Israel who has done all these things.

Again, in the book of Zechariah the Lord reveals His plan for Jerusalem and His people.

> *Thus says the LORD of hosts, "I am exceedingly jealous for Zion, (Jerusalem), yes, with great wrath I am jealous for her." Thus says the LORD, "I will return to Zion and will dwell in the midst of Jerusalem. Then Jerusalem will be called the City of Truth, and the mountain of the LORD of hosts will be called the Holy Mountain."*
> *Zechariah 8:2-3*

The Lord Himself declares that in the last days with *"great wrath He is jealous for Zion"* (Jerusalem). His wrath is the cup of reeling that the nations will be forced to drink if they persist in seeking to divide His holy city. He will return soon and dwell in the midst of Jerusalem, and His Mountain will be called the Holy Mountain.

The Messiah, the Holy One of Israel is coming soon. There is no doubt as to where He will dwell, and what He will do upon His return.

> *"Sing for joy and be glad, O daughter of Zion; for behold I am coming and I will dwell in your midst," declares the LORD. "And many nations will join themselves to the LORD in that day and will become My people. Then I will dwell in your midst, and you will know that the LORD of hosts has sent Me to you. And the LORD will possess Judah as His portion in the holy land, and will again choose Jerusalem. Be silent, all flesh, before the LORD; for He is aroused from His holy habitation."*
> *Zechariah 2:10-13*

The Lord *is* coming. He *will* dwell in the midst of Judah (Israel) as His portion in the Holy Land, and He will again choose **Jerusalem!**

Woe to the nations who seek to lift the stone of Jerusalem from its rightful place before the return of the Lord.

Let the nations of the earth and their leaders tremble for the Lord has declared what He will do to those who seek to divide and lift Jerusalem from its rightful place.

"Be silent, all flesh, before the LORD; for He is aroused from His holy habitation."

CHAPTER 19

ONE NATION UNDER GOD

America is called the "land of the free and the home of the brave." In the Pledge of Allegiance to the Flag, America is described as, "One nation under God."

America's founding fathers chose to base the Constitution and the Bill of Rights upon the Judeo-Christian principles of the word of the Living God. These principles, all of which are found in the Bible, caused America to come forth as a nation that was truly "under God."

America has been incredibly blessed for over 226 years because our nation was founded on the principle that we acknowledge that our blessings flow from God, not from man, and we look to Him, not to man, to lead us and guide us as a nation.

What does being "one nation under God really mean?"

"One nation under God" simply means that the people of a nation know their God, know His word and they are obedient to follow His commandments and His teachings.

"One nation under God," is a nation whose values are reflected in its laws, in the lives of its government leaders, and in the individual lives of each citizen.

THE BATTLE FOR THE SOUL OF AMERICA

There is an age-old battle taking place in America today, between the kingdom of God and the kingdom of Satan (the devil). God and His Son, Jesus Christ, represent the kingdom of God and all that is light and holy, while Satan and his demons represent the kingdom of Satan and all that is dark and evil.

Today in America, there are those who represent both kingdoms - the kingdom of God and His Son, and the kingdom of Satan. Jesus said this plainly.

"Any kingdom divided against itself is laid waste; and any city or house divided against itself will not stand." Matthew 12:25

In this verse, you might say that Jesus could be describing America. The division tearing our nation apart is a spiritual division that goes to the very foundation of our existence as a nation. The outcome of this battle holds the key to our nation's future!

To the victor goes the soul of our nation!

The battle that is being fought today for the soul of America is far more deadly than the one that has been launched against us by the Islamic Fundamentalists. We will either remain "One nation under God," or we will turn away and become "One nation under Satan."

Satan is working against America just as he is working against Israel. Both nations have enemies attacking them from without and from within. Our enemies have one ultimate goal, the complete destruction of America and Israel.

WHOM DO YOU WORSHIP – GOD OR SATAN?

Satan, the Prince of darkness revealed that worship is what this ancient battle is all about, because whomever you worship and serve is your god!

This eternal proof was confirmed when the Holy Spirit led Jesus Christ up into the wilderness to be tempted and tested by Satan, as recorded in the Bible in the New Testament book of Luke.

And he (Satan) led Him up and showed Him all the kingdoms of the world in a moment of time. And the devil said to Him, "I will give You all this domain and its glory; for it has been handed over to me, and I give it to whomever I wish. <u>Therefore if You worship before me, it shall all be Yours.</u>" Luke 4:5-7

In these verses, Satan showed Jesus all the kingdoms of the world and after showing them to Jesus, Satan said to Him,

"I will give you all this domain and its glory for it has been handed over to me, and I give it to whomever I wish."

The only requirement for Jesus to possess Satan's kingdom was to bow down and *worship* him!

Notice that Jesus did not dispute Satan's claim that he had been given dominion over *"All the kingdoms of the world."* Jesus did not dispute Satan's claim, because it is true! Yet how did Jesus answer Satan?

Jesus replied, "It is written, 'You shall worship the Lord your God and serve Him only!'" Luke 4:8

The central issue for you, for me and for the United States today is no different than it was for Jesus Christ. Each of us must decide whom we will worship! Let there be clear understanding concerning this issue, there are only two kingdoms, the kingdom of God and the kingdom of Satan. All of us worship and serve one or the other whether we realize it or not!

To those who say, "There is no God", what they are actually doing in denying God is acknowledging and becoming a part of the kingdom of Satan. There is no neutral kingdom. You are either in one kingdom or the other whether you like it or not!

Jesus could not have stated it more clearly.

"He who is not with Me is against Me; and he who does not gather with Me, scatters." Luke 11:23

In which kingdom you will spend your eternity, whether in the kingdom of God or in the kingdom of Satan, is determined by the choice you make as to whom you are "with" or whom you are "against". Understand clearly, your eternal fate will be determined by whom you choose to serve and worship.

Understanding of this issue is central to the battle being fought for the heart and soul of America today. A nation as a people, are either for the Lord or against Him! There is no middle ground in this battle. And before America and you make your choice you should know that, in the

153

end, only one kingdom will prevail and that *will* be the Kingdom of God and of His Son Jesus Christ!

America and her people cannot declare in the Pledge of Allegiance to the flag that they are "One Nation under God," when prayer to God has been effectively eliminated from the public schools.

America and her people cannot imprint on the nation's currency, "In God We Trust," when the nation has effectively eliminated the displaying and teaching of God's Ten Commandments in the nation's schools and on public property.

America and her people cannot claim to be "One nation under God," when the land is stained with the blood of millions of aborted, innocent babies.

America and her people cannot ask "God to Bless America," when the schools teach the children there is no God, thus they need not pray to Him nor obey His commandments!

America and her people cannot sing "God Bless America," when the teaching of, *"In the beginning God created the heavens and earth,"* to her children has all but been eliminated from the public schools.

America was founded on the principles of the Ten Commandments and the Bible, and these commandments are an integral part of the Judeo-Christian foundation of America. But America is steadily turning her back on this foundation and is undermining the stability of her future and her very existence as a nation.

On June 26, 2002, in a 2-1 decision, the 9th U.S. Circuit Court of Appeals declared for the first time that reciting the Pledge of Allegiance in public schools is unconstitutional because of the words "under God" inserted by Congress in 1954.

Leading schoolchildren in a pledge that says the United States is "one nation under God" is as objectionable as making them say "we are a nation 'under Jesus', a nation 'under Vishnu', a nation 'under Zeus', or a nation 'under no god', because none of these professions can be neutral with respect to religion," Circuit Judge Alfred T. Goodwin wrote.

The Supreme Court supposedly begins each of its sessions with the phrase 'God save the United States and this honorable court', yet this cannot be done in the nation's schools.

What will be the next target of the "prophets of Jezebel"? Possibly, the Declaration of Independence will be declared unconstitutional because it refers to God or to the creator four different times. Possibly our Congress, which begins each session with a prayer, will be forbidden to mention the name of God, and we can expect that the words 'In God We Trust' may be removed from our nations currency.

AMERICA - TRUTH VS. DECEPTION

TRUTH

Ah, the age-old question ... what is truth?

Over the last 25 years our nation's courts have effectively eliminated the teaching from the nation's public schools that God created the heavens and the earth, as the Bible declares. Our school system teaches Darwin's theory of Evolution, which declares we evolved from monkeys.

But what does the word of God have to say on this issue?

> *In the beginning God created the heavens and the earth. And God created man in His own image, male and female He created them. God saw all that He had made, and behold, it was very good. And there was evening and there was morning, the sixth day. THUS the heavens and the earth were completed, and all their hosts. By the seventh day God completed His work which He had done, and He rested on the seventh day from all His work which He had done. Genesis 1:1, 27, 31; 2:1-2*

From these verses we can easily see that the wisdom of man and the word of God are in direct opposition to one another. What is the truth then? Is it the word of God as written in the Bible, or is it the word and wisdom of man?

Ask yourself once again, are we truly "One nation under God?" Do the rulings of our courts give evidence that our nation, our leaders and we as individuals honor and seek God in the laws we embrace and enforce? Or it is evidence that we have chosen to utterly reject God and His word?

Either the Bible, the word of God as written in Scripture is true, or the word of man as espoused by such men as Darwin is. Each of us must choose which we will believe ... there is no middle ground on this most fundamental issue.

It is interesting to note that God says He created the heavens and the earth and everything in them in both the Old and the New Testaments,

> *"It is I who made the earth, and created man upon it. I stretched out the heavens with My hands And I ordained all their host. Isaiah 45:12*

> *"Worthy are You, our Lord and our God, to receive glory and honor and power; for You created all things, and because of Your will they existed, and were created." Revelation 4:11*

Nowhere is the contrast starker, the differences more clear than over this issue. God either exists and He is the creator as He has clearly said, or He does not exist and we are all here by accident and evolution. Where do *you* stand on this foundational issue? Do you stand with the word of man or do you stand with the word of God?

> *"I have heard what the prophets have said who prophesy falsely in My name, saying, 'I had a dream, I had a dream!' How long? Is there anything in the hearts of the prophets who prophesy falsehood, even these prophets of the deception of their own heart, who intend to make My people forget My name by their dreams which they relate to one another, just as their fathers forgot My name because of Baal? The prophet who has a dream may relate his dream, but let him who has My word speak My word in truth. What does straw have in common with grain?" declares the Lord. Jeremiah 23:25-28*

We see in these verses that the purpose of the "false" prophet is found in the deception of their own hearts, and that their intent is to make God's people forget His name. They do not speak the word of God in truth. They speak lies from the deception of their own hearts.

Who does Jesus say is a liar and the father of lies?

> *"... the devil, he is a liar and the father of lies." John 8:44*

The word of God declares,

> *"In the beginning God created the heavens and the earth." Genesis 1:1*

What is the truth?

> *"... Thy Word is truth." John 17:17*

DECEPTION

SEE THAT NO ONE DECEIVES YOU!

Jesus was asked by His disciples while sitting on the Mount of Olives, "What will be the sign of your return?" His answer in Matthew 24 is most enlightening.

> *"See to it that no one misleads (deceives) you."*
> *Matthew 24:4*

Why did Jesus choose to answer His disciples in this way? Jesus was revealing to them, as well as to you and me, that one of the first signs of His return, or 2nd coming, will be a time when the spirit of deception is so strong upon the earth that even the saints (Jesus' believers or followers) could be overtaken by it.

Notice that the first and most important sign regarding the second coming of Jesus Christ, the Messiah, dealt with the *condition* of man's heart. Prior to His return would be a time when men's hearts would be filled with lies, half-truths, distortions, deception and every manner of

157

evil, just like they were in the days of Noah. That is why Jesus warns us to *not* be deceived.

> *"For the coming of the Son of Man will be just like the days of Noah." Matthew 24:37*

How does the word of God describe the days of Noah?

> *Then the LORD saw that the wickedness of man was great on the earth, and that every intent of the thoughts of his heart was only evil continually. Now the earth was corrupt in the sight of God, and the earth was filled with violence. God looked on the earth, and behold, it was corrupt; for all flesh had corrupted their way upon the earth. Genesis 6:5, 11-12*

The apostle Paul accurately described the times in which we live thousands of years ago in 2 Timothy, Chapter 3. See if it doesn't read and sound like our 6 o'clock news today.

> *But realize this, that in the last days difficult times will come. For men will be lovers of self, lovers of money, boastful, arrogant, revilers, disobedient to parents, ungrateful, unholy, unloving, irreconcilable, malicious gossips, without self-control, brutal, haters of good, treacherous, reckless, conceited, lovers of pleasure rather than lovers of God, holding to a form of godliness, although they have denied its power; Avoid such men as these. II Timothy 3:1-5*

There are no exceptions with God. Human history is living testimony that He means exactly what He says in His word. When Israel was disobedient He did exactly what He said He would do if they did not obey His commandments. Notice that all of the characteristics in these verses deal with the *condition* of man's heart.

In the last days, why will the deception be so strong and so much evil on the earth? Because Satan will be exercising all the powers at his command to lead people *away* from worshiping and following the Lord and *into* worshiping and following him.

Understand that the battle being fought today in America and in the world is over one issue. **Whom do you worship – God or Satan?**

Ask yourself; do you live in a nation where this deception is strong? Are you living in a time when men are lovers of self, lovers of money, boastful and arrogant? Do you live in a time when children are disobedient to parents, ungrateful, unholy, unloving and often irreconcilable?

Ask yourself, when you watch the 6 o'clock news, do you see many who are without self-control, brutal, haters of good, treacherous and reckless? Do you live in a time when people are lovers of pleasure rather than lovers of God, holding to a form of godliness, although they have denied its power?

Ask yourself, what is the condition of *your* heart? Do you love the *Lord* or the things of the *world?* Whom do *you* worship and serve?

The Apostle Paul reminded us in these verses that when you see these things in the world around you, know and understand that we are living in difficult times and we have entered the period in human history known as the **last days.**

HISTORY SHOWS US THAT GOD MEANS EXACTLY WHAT HE SAYS IN HIS WORD

The Lord warned Israel about the consequences of disobedience to His commandments in the Old Testament book of Deuteronomy. Hundreds of years later, when they were disobedient, He fulfilled His word to the last jot and tittle.

Because of Israel's disobedience, the Lord sent the Roman general Titus in 70 A.D. to conquer Jerusalem and Judah. He destroyed Jerusalem and the Temple, and dispersed the Jews throughout the nations of the earth, where they remained scattered for 2,000 years.

"Moreover, the LORD will scatter you among all peoples, from one end of the earth to the other end of the earth; and there you shall serve other gods, wood and stone, which you or your fathers have not known. Among those nations you shall find no rest, and there will be no resting place for the sole of your foot; but there the LORD will give you a trembling heart, failing of eyes, and despair of soul. So your life shall hang in doubt before you; and you will be in dread night and day, and shall have no assurance of your life." Deuteronomy 28:64-66

The Lord does not keep His plans secret, nor does He conceal the consequences of sin. They are plainly stated in His word. America is no longer "One nation under God," and the Lord is going to deal with her just as He dealt with Israel and just as He will with any nation who disobeys His commandments.

Remember the mighty former Soviet Union? It was the second most powerful nation on earth at the time of its utter collapse. It fell without a shot being fired because they would not heed the Word of the Lord to, *"Let My people go!"* Is America any different? Will God view us any differently when we turn away and disobey Him and His word?

What is true for a nation is equally true for us as individuals. Jesus said,

"If you love Me, you will keep My commandments."
John 14:15

Jesus equated loving Him with keeping His commandments. He further supported this teaching in John, Chapter 14.

"He who has My commandments and keeps them is the one who loves Me; and he who loves Me will be loved by My Father, and I will love him and will disclose Myself to him." John 14:21

Jesus, the Son of the God of the Old Testament, is telling us that the one who loves Him (Jesus) is the one who keeps *His commandments*, and will be loved by His Father (God), and He will disclose Himself to those who love Him.

160

Some would declare that the Ten Commandments are part of the Old Testament, and as Christians, they are not under the Old Covenant (or Old Testament). Yet, what did Jesus say about the law and the prophets?

> *"Do not think that I came to abolish the Law or the Prophets; I did not come to abolish but to fulfill. For truly I say to you, until heaven and earth pass away, not the smallest letter or stroke shall pass from the Law until all is accomplished." Matthew 5:17-18*

The Lord is revealing that there is one true test that reveals if we are a people who know their God, and if we are in fact, "One nation under God." The test is "our obedience and faithfulness to keep His commandments."

Plainly, Jesus is declaring that if a nation or a people *do not* keep His commandments they are liars, and the truth is not in them.

> *The one who says, "I have come to know Him," and does not keep His commandments, is a liar, and the truth is not in him; but whoever keeps His word, in him the love of God has truly been perfected. By this we know that we are in Him." I John 2:4-5*

THE LORD IS CALLING HIS PEOPLE BACK TO HIM

When the Lord brought Israel out of Egypt, He did it for a very specific purpose.

> *And the Lord said, "Certainly I will be with you, and this shall be the sign to you that it is I who have sent you: when you have brought the people out of Egypt, <u>you shall worship God at this mountain</u>." Exodus 3:12*

God's primary purpose for Israel is revealed in these wonderful verses. He brought the Israelites out of Egypt for the specific purpose of "worshiping Him." Only through worshiping God would they have a heart to obey His Commandments and teach them to their children.

161

A HOLY NATION AND A KINGDOM OF PRIESTS

Worshiping God gave Israel a heart to obey God, and it was through worship that they became His possession. Only then could they become a kingdom of priests and a holy nation before the Lord.

> *" 'Now then, if you will indeed obey My voice and keep My covenant, then you shall be My own possession among all the peoples, for all the earth is Mine; and you shall be to Me a kingdom of priests and a holy nation.' These are the words that you shall speak to the sons of Israel."*
> *Exodus 19:5-6*

God's ultimate purpose for Israel is to be His own possession, and to be a kingdom of priests, a holy nation who worships Him and obeys His commandments.

And what did Jesus Christ declare regarding the ultimate purpose for His church here on earth?

> *But you are a chosen race, a royal priesthood, a holy nation, a people for God's own possession, so that you may proclaim the excellencies of Him who has called you out of darkness into His marvelous light; for you once were not a people, but now you are the people of God; you had not received mercy, but now you have received mercy.*
> *I Peter 2:9-10*

It is really quite interesting to note in comparing the above verses that the callings of God the Father to Israel, and the callings of Jesus Christ, the Son, to His church, are *exactly* the same callings. Those who follow the Lord are truly called as a *"chosen race"*. But, "chosen" for what?

Both are called to be *"a holy nation"* and a *"royal priesthood"* to live as examples among a people who are not walking in the way of the Lord. Both have been chosen to be *"the people of God"* because *"they have received the mercy of God."*

Do we not all need the mercy of God in our lives?

Do we not all need the mercy of God on our nation?

How can America be a royal priesthood, a nation of priests, when it is a nation that worships the wisdom of man, the glory of man, the knowledge of man, and the power of man?

America is a nation that has been exceedingly, abundantly blessed by God. But, America is a nation that has forgotten God. America is a nation that has become arrogant and rebellious against God.

As a nation, America's courts are seeking to remove "One nation under God," from the Pledge of Allegiance, to dismiss Him from the courts, to effectively remove Him from our public institutions, to expel Him from the schools, to remove God and His Ten Commandments from our schools and public places, so as to separate our people and our nation from their God.

While our courts seek to remove The Ten Commandments from government property and from our national life, what does the Lord command us to do?

> *"And you shall love the Lord your God with all your heart, and with all your soul and with all your might. And these words, which I am commanding you today, shall be on your heart; and you shall teach them diligently to your sons and shall talk of them when you sit in your house and when you walk by the way and when you lie down and when you rise up." Deuteronomy 6:5-7*

Ask yourself, is America truly "One Nation Under God?"

CHAPTER 20

BIRTH PANGS

Every woman who has given birth has experienced "birth pangs". They start slowly, and they increase in intensity and frequency until the only thing that will cause the birth pangs to stop is the birth of the baby.

Jesus used the term "birth pangs" to describe what the world would be like prior to His return. He sought to give us clear insight so we could recognize some of the physical signs that would appear on earth just before His return.

One cannot understand the world today when we look at events through human eyes, and through our limited human wisdom. World and national events simply make no sense.

To understand events taking place in America, Israel and the world today, we need spiritual wisdom and insight.

> *"You will be hearing of wars and rumors of wars. See that you are not frightened, for those things must take place, but that is not yet the end. For nation will rise against nation, and kingdom against kingdom, and in various places there will be famines and earthquakes, But all these things are merely the beginning of birth pangs."*
> *Matthew 24:6-8*

Look at the nightly news. Would you not agree that we are living in a time when the world is filled with "birth pangs"? Are we not living in a time when nation is rising against nation? Has not the kingdom of Islam risen up against many kingdoms?

WORLD CONFLICTS AT THE BEGINNING OF 2002

All across our planet there is conflict, war, terror, violence and famine. There are some thirty major conflicts in the world today between or within nations. Of these thirty major conflicts, twenty-eight of them, over 93%, involve Islamic fundamentalists. The kingdom of Islam is rising and executing its plan to conquer and dominate the world. The kingdom of Islam has risen up against all nations who will not bow down and worship their god – Allah. Look at the continents that dot our planet. There are wars and conflicts on every continent and in every part of the world.

Europe & the Balkans:
Cyprus – conflicts between Greeks and Turks
Kosovo – Serbia
Serbian/Yugoslav Government vs. Ethnic Albanian
Northern Ireland
Spain
Bosnia
Macedonians vs. Albanians

Asia and the Pacific:
India vs. Pakistan,
America vs. Afghanistan
Kashmir – India vs. Pakistan
Thailand vs. Myanmar
Burma
Sri Lanka
North Korea vs. South Korea
China vs. Taiwan
East Timor - Indonesia
Philippines

Africa:
In the Sudan, a Muslim-led civil war has been raging for decades in which over two million Sudanese Christians have been killed, wounded or enslaved by this Muslim regime.
Algeria
Angola
Congo – Zaire
Nigeria
Zimbabwe

Middle East:
Israel vs. Palestinians
Israel vs. Iraq
Israel vs. Syria

Israel vs. Saudi Arabia
America vs. Iraq & Iran
Turkey vs. Kurdistan
Ethiopia

The Americas:
Columbia
Peru & Argentina
Mexico – Chiapas

Christians by the hundreds of thousands have been killed in the Sudan, Ethiopia, Indonesia and the Philippines. Many are in prison in Saudi Arabia.

In Malaysia, the Philippines, and Pakistan there are Muslims who are capturing and killing people for no reason other than the fact that they are Christian by faith.

WHY IS ISLAM AT THE CENTER OF SO MANY OF THESE CONFLICTS?

Islam is not a peaceful religion. It is a religion of domination and does not tolerate other religions. Those religions that it cannot control and dominate it must destroy. Islam is very much like the "spirit of Jezebel" in that it cannot "cohabitate with" other religions.

Islam dominates from within and without and America took notice of this fact only after September 11th. The video and newspaper images of life in Afghanistan under the Muslim-led Taliban regime gave naïve Americans an unprecedented insight into an Islamic fundamentalist society.

The words of the Koran speak for themselves on this point.

Sura 2:191 – (Instructing Muslims to fight those who fight them) - "Kill them, (Jews and Christians),_wherever you find them, and turn them out from where they have turned you out."

Sura 9:5 – (Refers to Christians and Jews and to kill them) – "Then, when the sacred months have passed, slay the idolaters, (Christians and Jews) wherever ye find them, and take them captive and besiege them and prepare for them an ambush."

Sura 9:123 "Fight those of the unbelievers who are near to you, and let them find harshness in you, and know that Allah is with those who serve him."

Sura 9:30 "The Christians say: The Christ is the son of Allah; these are the words of their mouths; they imitate the saying of those who disbelieved before; may Allah destroy them."

Sura 23.91 (The God who sent His Son into the world to save it cannot be the same god who inspired Muhammad to write) - "NEVER DID ALLAH TAKE TO HIMSELF A SON, and never was there with him any (other) god."

Sura 17.111 "All praise is due to Allah, WHO HAS NOT TAKEN A SON and WHO HAS NOT A PARTNER in the kingdom."

WHAT DID THE APOSTLE JOHN SAY REGARDING THOSE WHO DENY THE FATHER AND THE SON?

"Who is the liar but the one who denies that Jesus is the Christ? This is the antichrist, the one who denies the Father and the Son. Whoever denies the Son does not have the Father; the one who confesses the Son has the Father also." I John 2:22-23

The word of God declares that because they deny the Father and the Son, Islam and the Koran are the spirit of the antichrist.

"By this you know the Spirit of God: every spirit that confesses that Jesus Christ has come in the flesh is from God; and every spirit that does not confess Jesus is not from God; this is the spirit of the antichrist, of which you have heard that it is coming, and now it is already in the world." I John 4:2-3

The Koran of Islam directly contradicts and attacks some of the most basic and essential truths of the Judeo-Christian faith. There is nothing out of context about these verses. They represent the consistent theme of the Koran's teaching about God the Father and Jesus the Son as well as the instructions to its followers on how to deal with those outside the religion of Islam, particularly the Jew and the Christian.

Jesus said that we should all "recognize the signs of the times." We need only watch the news or pick up a newspaper to see that the "spirit of the antichrist" that Jesus warned us about, is alive and well in the world today and that the "birth pangs" signaling the end of the age are increasing in frequency and intensity.

CHAPTER 21

THE BATTLE BETWEEN TWO KINGDOMS

The colossal spiritual battle taking place in America today between the kingdom of God and the kingdom of Satan can be viewed in the ancient battle described in the Bible between the "Spirit of Elijah" and the "spirit of Jezebel."

In this age-old battle, *"Elijah"* represents the Spirit of God and His Son. The "spirit of Jezebel" represents "the unique power and principality" whose purpose it is to lead the people away from the worship of God to the worship of Satan and the idols of man. The Bible tells us that the "power of Jezebel" led all the kings of the northern Kingdom of Israel away from the worship of the God of Israel into the idolatrous worship of other gods. This same subtle spirit is quite able today to lead Americans away from the worship of the One True and Living God into the idolatrous worship of other gods.

Every American understood the attack launched by the Islamic fundamentalists on September 11th, because it was a physical attack, terrifying and violent. Yet, there is another attack underway that is far more deadly than a physical battle. It is part of an ancient and historic war that is being fought today for the very soul of the American people.

And if this war is lost, America is lost!

AGAINST WHOM AND WHAT DO WE FIGHT?

Understanding with whom and against what it is that we are really fighting is the key to understanding how to win this battle. The Apostle Paul gave us great insight into this issue in the book of Ephesians.

> *For our struggle is not against flesh and blood, but against the rulers, against the powers, against the world forces of this darkness, against the spiritual forces of wickedness in the heavenly places. Ephesians 6:12*

Flesh and blood represent the physical manifestation of what is taking place in the spiritual realm. We are engaged in a spiritual battle for the souls of our husbands and wives, for the souls of our children and grandchildren, for the souls of our nation's leaders and for the soul of our nation as a people.

Our battle is against powers and principalities. Our battle is against spiritual forces of wickedness which we cannot see. Our battle is more real and more deadly than one thousand hydrogen bombs!

Jesus described these powers.

> *"Do not fear those who kill the body but are unable to kill the soul; but rather fear Him who is able to destroy both soul and body in hell." Matthew 10:28.*

One of the most powerful "spiritual principalities" we war against is called "the spiritual power of Jezebel."

Much can be learned by careful study of this ancient battle fought between the "spirit of Elijah" and the "spiritual power of Jezebel" as it applies to America.

What does the name Jezebel mean? It is interesting to note that the name "Jezebel" means "without cohabitation." Simply translated, this means that this spirit refuses to live together with anyone unless it can control and dominate the relationship. This spirit yields to no one!

It should be understood that "spiritual powers" are not people and they are genderless. Therefore, they influence and control both men and women.

Islam is a religion filled with the "spiritual power of Jezebel" in that it cannot cohabitate, or live together, with any people or nation unless Islam controls and dominates that society or nation.

The "spirit of Islam," yields to no one!

170

In the Bible, and following in the footsteps of the prophet Samuel, the prophet Elijah was head of the school of prophets in the northern kingdom of Israel. Under Elijah were the hundreds of prophets whose duty it was to proclaim the word of the Lord to the Jewish people.

The "spiritual power of Jezebel" operating through Queen Jezebel caused the entire northern Kingdom of Israel (the northern 10 tribes) to turn from their covenant with the God of Israel, destroy the sacred altars, kill the prophets of God and bow down and worship the idols Baal and Asherah.

The power of this spirit was so strong that it caused the prophet Elijah to cry out to God in 1 Kings.

> *Then he said, "I have been very zealous for the LORD, the God of hosts; for the sons of Israel have forsaken Your covenant, torn down Your altars and killed Your prophets with the sword. And I alone am left; and they seek my life, to take it away." I Kings 19:14*

The "spiritual power of Jezebel" is fiercely independent, ambitious for pre-eminence and control and utilizes the weapons of murder, terror, intimidation, war and fear against its opponents.

When Queen Jezebel married King Ahab, she soon began to dominate him. By usurping his authority, she set about to systematically murder all of God's prophets and servants in the northern Kingdom of Israel.

Why would Queen Jezebel seek to murder and silence the prophets of the God of Israel? She sought their destruction because she wanted to destroy everyone who spoke and taught the commandments of the God of Israel.

You shall have no other God's before Me.
You shall not worship nor bow down to idols.
You shall not murder.
You shall not covet thy neighbor's wife or anything that is thy neighbors.
You shall keep the Sabbath day.
You shall obey My commandments.

Queen Jezebel murdered the prophets of the God of Israel so she could replace them with the ungodly prophets of Baal. She filled her palace and all the surrounding worship centers with 450 priests and 400 priestesses to a foreign god.

So, when we speak of the "spiritual power of Jezebel," we are describing that "unique principality" or spiritual source in our society that the Apostle Paul called "the powers and principalities of Satan."

These powers and principalities are using human agents in our midst. Those human agents are revealed by their words and actions and have one primary function: To lead the nation away from serving and worshiping the One True and Living God, and into serving and worshiping Satan and the things of his kingdom.

THE SPIRITUAL POWERS AND PRINCIPALITIES HAVE LED OUR NATION TO EFFECTIVELY REMOVE PRAYER TO GOD FROM OUR NATIONS SCHOOLS

The "spiritual power of Jezebel", operating through the court system has effectively removed public prayer from the public schools. Notice that the "spiritual power of Jezebel" has influenced the courts to seek to remove "One nation under God," and the Pledge of Allegiance from the schools and national life.

Just as in the days of Elijah, all of the nation's teachers who believe in God are being silenced and rarely speak, teach about, or pray to God openly in the schools.

The "spiritual power of Jezebel", is responsible for leading the American people away from praying and worshiping God, and into the worship of the wisdom of man.

Think about it. When did this all begin? It began with the assault by the "prophets of Jezebel," who sought to remove prayer and The Ten Commandments from the nation's schools.

The "prophets of Jezebel," have successfully made a separation between America's people and their god!

BEHOLD, the LORD'S hand is not so short that it cannot save; nor is His ear so dull that it cannot hear. But your iniquities have made a separation between you and your God, and your sins have hidden His face from you so that He does not hear. Isaiah 59:1-2

Sadly, America, has become like the northern Kingdom of Israel, in which the "spiritual power of Jezebel" is leading her people to worship the wisdom of man and away from worshiping the True and the Living God. Ah, the wisdom of man!

Ahab the son of Omri did evil in the sight of the LORD more than all who were before him. It came about, <u>as though it had been a trivial thing</u> for him to walk in the sins of Jeroboam the son of Nebat, that he married Jezebel the daughter of Ethbaal king of the Sidonians, <u>and went to serve Baal and worshiped him</u>.
I Kings 16:30-31.

Jezebel was a Phoenician Princess, and her marriage to Ahab, king of the northern Kingdom of Israel, was a political alliance between two nations. She grew up worshiping the idol Baal, and once she had married Ahab, she was determined to drive Jehovah God of Israel out.

Single-handedly using murder, threats and intimidation, she caused the entire northern Kingdom of Israel to abandon the God of Israel and worship and bow down to the idol Baal.

We read from the verses above the words, "<u>as though it had been a trivial thing</u>" to walk in the sins of Jeroboam, marry Jezebel and serve Baal and worship him.

WAS IT A TRIVIAL THING TO REMOVE PRAYER FROM OUR SCHOOLS ?

Is it a trivial thing to effectively remove the teaching and display of The Ten Commandments from the schools and nation's public property?

Is it a trivial thing for the schools to effectively teach the children there is no creator, therefore there is no God?

173

Is a trivial thing that the courts are seeking to remove "One nation under God," from the Pledge of Allegiance?

Is a trivial thing to sing "God Bless America," when we have effectively removed the teaching of His Ten Commandments from the nation's schools and public property?

OUR INIQUITIES HAVE SEPARATED US FROM OUR GOD

But your iniquities have made a separation between you and your God, and your sins have hidden His face from you so that He does not hear. Isaiah 59:2

Can anything be worse than separation from our God so that He does not hear our prayers? What will be the fate of America if the Lord has hidden His face from her?

For our transgressions are multiplied before You, And our sins testify against us; For our transgressions are with us, And we know our iniquities: Transgressing and denying the LORD, And turning away from our God, Speaking oppression and revolt, Conceiving in and uttering from the heart lying words. Justice is turned back, And righteousness stands far away; For truth has stumbled in the street, And uprightness cannot enter. Yes, truth is lacking; And he who turns aside from evil makes himself a prey. Isaiah 59:12-15

Our sins testify against us and we know our iniquities because we are transgressing and denying the Lord. Because we have turned away from our God, justice is turned back and truth is lacking.

America's future as a nation hangs in the balance. She has become like the northern Kingdom of Israel. She has abandoned God and has bowed down to worship another.

In the days ahead, the soul of the nation along with the soul of every man, woman and child living in America, shall be weighed upon a scale of worship.

Each of us must make the individual decision of whom we choose to bow down and worship, God or Satan? The outcome will determine the destiny of our eternal souls as well as the eternal destiny of the great nation of America.

A SCHOOL PRINCIPAL SPEAKS OUT

This is a statement that was read over the public address system at a football game at Roane County Christian High School in Kingston, Tennessee by school Principal Jody McLoud, on September 1, 2000. It shows just how far our country has gone in the wrong direction.

"It has always been the custom at Roane County High School football games to say a prayer and play the National Anthem to honor God and Country. **Due to a recent ruling by the Supreme Court, I am told that saying a prayer is a violation of Federal Case Law.**

As I understand the law at this time, I can use this public facility to approve of sexual perversion and call it "an alternate lifestyle" and if someone is offended, that's OK.

I can use it to condone sexual promiscuity by dispensing condoms and calling it "safe sex" and if someone is offended, that's OK.

I can even use this public facility to present the merits of killing an unborn baby as a "viable means of birth control."

I can designate a school day as "Earth Day" and involve students in activities to worship religiously and praise the goddess "Mother Earth" and call it "ecology" and if someone is offended, that's OK.

I can use literature, videos and presentations in the classroom that depict people with strong, traditional Christian convictions as "simple minded" and "ignorant" and call it, "enlightenment."

However, if anyone uses this facility to honor God, and to ask Him to bless this event with safety and good sportsmanship, then a Federal Case Law is violated.

This appears to be inconsistent at best, and at worst, diabolical. Apparently, we are to be tolerant of everything and anyone, except God and His Commandments.

Nevertheless, as a school principal, I frequently ask staff and students to abide by rules with which they do not necessarily agree. For me to do otherwise, would be inconsistent at best, and at worst, hypocritical. I suffer from that affliction enough unintentionally. I certainly do not need to add an intentional transgression.

For this reason, I shall "Render unto Caesar that which is Caesar's," and refrain from praying at this time.

However, if you feel inspired to honor, praise and thank God, and ask Him, in the name of Jesus, to bless this event, please feel free to do so. As far as I know, that's not against the law ---- yet."

One by one, the people in the stands bowed their heads, held hands with one another, and began to pray. They prayed in the stands. They prayed in the team huddles. They prayed at the concession stand, and they prayed in the announcer's box. The only place they didn't pray was in the Supreme Court of the United States of America - the seat of "justice" in the "One nation, under God."

Somehow, Kingston, Tennessee remembered what so many have forgotten. We are given the Freedom **OF** Religion, not the Freedom **FROM** Religion.

Praise God that His remnant remains!

CHAPTER 22

THOU SHALT HAVE NO OTHER GODS BEFORE ME

God said it plainly in The Ten Commandments given to Moses in Exodus.

> *"You shall have no other gods before Me." You shall not make for yourself an idol, or any likeness of what is in heaven above or on the earth beneath or in the water under the earth. You shall not worship them or serve them; for I, the LORD your God, am a jealous God, visiting the iniquity of the fathers on the children, on the third and the fourth generations of those who hate Me, but showing lovingkindness to thousands, to those who love Me and keep My commandments." Exodus 20:3-6*

THE UNITED STATES SUPREME COURT REJECTS APPEAL ON TEN COMMANDMENTS

CNN (Cable News Network) reported on February 25, 2002 that the U.S. Supreme Court refused to consider an appeal in the state of Indiana seeking permission to erect on the statehouse grounds in Indianapolis, a seven-foot stone monument bearing The Ten Commandments.

Without any comment or dissent, the justices let stand a federal appeals court ruling, contending that placing the monument on government property would violate separation of church and state under the U.S. Constitution's First Amendment.

The appeals court held that The Ten Commandments contained an inherently religious text, and that the proposed monument amounted to an endorsement of religion by the state.

Lawyers for the Indiana Civil Liberties Union opposed the appeal, stating the posting of the text of The Ten Commandments was not a memorial "to a common secular heritage."

Posting a document like this that is sacred to Christians and Jews is directly contrary to what this court has reputed to be our "real heritage". Yet, what did the Lord command all of Israel to do regarding His commandments? What *is* America's "real heritage"?

THOU SHALL TEACH MY COMMANDMENTS TO YOUR CHILDREN

> *"Hear, O Israel! The LORD is our God, the LORD is one! You shall love the LORD your God with all your heart and with all your soul and with all your might. These words, which I am commanding you today, shall be on your heart. You shall teach them diligently to your sons and shall talk of them when you sit in your house and when you walk by the way and when you lie down and when you rise up." Deuteronomy 6:4-7*

America's *heritage* was based upon teaching her children God's Ten Commandments. America's *heritage* was based upon teaching her children to love the Lord their God with all their hearts, souls, strength and mind. America's *heritage* was based upon the prayer and song, "God Bless America!"

The "the spiritual power of Jezebel" in our midst, who worships the wisdom of man and serves the kingdom of Satan, has brought forth this mandate from the pit of hell.

Only the "wisdom of man", empowered by the "spiritual power of Jezebel", would be so arrogant as to assert that we do not need prayer in the schools nor do we need to teach God's Ten Commandments to the children.

The "spiritual power of Jezebel" has so pervaded and influenced the nation's judges that they are now espousing the greatest lie in the history of the United States by declaring: *"Posting a document holy to Jews and Christians is directly contrary to what this court has noted to be our real heritage."*

Notice, the "spiritual power of Jezebel" cannot "cohabitate" with the Living God and the teachings of the Living God. The "modern day prophets" of Jezebel who are presiding in our nation's courts have done

178

exactly what Queen Jezebel did to the prophets of the northern Kingdom of Israel.

These modern day "prophets of Jezebel" like the prophets of Ahab's time are seeking to "kill off the prophets of God" in America. They are seeking to replace The Ten Commandments and teachings of God with the commandments and the teaching of man.

These modern day "prophets of Jezebel" are using the power of the courts to silence the "Elijah's" of this generation who are the modern day prophets of God.

Why? Because like the prophets of old, they seek to declare the truth to a nation that is being led astray by false prophets to serve those who worship the wisdom of man, not the commandments of God.

Our nation will perish if we reject the knowledge of God and embrace the wisdom of man. The Ten Commandments are the most holy and important Judeo-Christian document ever written because it is God breathed and brings life to our people and to our nation.

> *My people perish for want of knowledge! Since you have rejected knowledge, I will reject you from my priesthood. Since you have forgotten the law of your God, I also will forget your children. Hosea 4:6*

America is perishing because we have rejected the knowledge of God and we are effectively seeking to remove Him from our schools, from our Pledge of Allegiance, and from our children, and from our national heritage as "One nation under God."

OUR GOD IS A JEALOUS GOD

The Bible tells us to seek our maker – to seek God with all your heart, with all your soul, with all your mind and with all your strength!

How are we to execute this commandment? We do it through living by and teaching His commandments to our children!

The Lord declared in The Ten Commandments that we are not to have or worship any other God for one reason, that He is a jealous God!

179

Can you believe it? We have a God who is jealous for our affection! Isn't that amazing? The Almighty God, creator of the heavens and the earth is jealous for our affection!

Here in this little verse is one of the greatest nuggets of the entire Bible. Our God is jealous because He wants us to love Him. He loved us so much that He made us in His image!

> *Then God said, "Let Us make man in Our image, according to Our likeness; and let them rule over the fish of the sea and over the birds of the sky and over the cattle and over all the earth, and over every creeping thing that creeps on the earth." Genesis 1:26*

In these first few verses of the Bible, we find the words, "Let US make man in Our image." Who is the "US" in this verse? Remember, these verses speak of a time in eternity when man did not exist. God cannot be speaking to angels because nowhere in Scripture does it say angels have the power to create anything.

It is an awesome thing to realize that we are made in the image of God. God is Spirit, and He has given us a spirit so we can commune with Him. God did not create us for only a moment in time but for all eternity. So everything He does in our lives has eternal significance.

So how do we get to know this awesome God, who is jealous for our affection and wants to have a personal relationship with you and me? How do we get close to Him, learn about Him, love Him and finally have a real relationship with Him? How do we come to know Him up close and personal as the one and only God? The golden key to this relationship is found in this one verse in the Bible,

> *For the Lord your God in the midst of you is a jealous God;...Deuteronomy 6:15*

He is jealous for our worship, jealous for our love, and jealous for us to obey His commandments and teach them to our children. His word declares that when we obey His commandments, and teach them diligently to our children, He will bless us, He will watch over us and He will give us eternal life!

HOW MUCH DOES GOD LOVE US?

For God so loved the world that He gave His only begotten Son, that whoever believes in Him shall not perish, but have eternal life. John 3:16

Our God, the same one who gave us The Ten Commandments, loved us so much that He sent His only Son, Jesus Christ to die on a cross as propitiation for our sins for one purpose: *"That we shall have eternal life!"*

America has become a people whose hearts are dull just like the hearts of Israel had become dull.

"For the heart of this people has become dull, with their ears they scarcely hear, and they have closed their eyes, Otherwise they would see with their eyes, Hear with their ears, and understand with their heart and return, And I would heal them." Isaiah 6:10

There is life in His Son, there is life in His Ten Commandments and there is life in His word! You can have that life! America can have that life. Any nation can have that life if only we'd return to the One True and Living God and obey His commandments!

JESUS DECLARES GOD'S JUDGMENT ON THOSE WHO KILL AND SILENCE THE PROPHETS OF GOD

"You serpents, you brood of vipers, how will you escape the sentence of hell? Therefore, behold, I am sending you prophets and wise men and scribes; some of them you will kill and crucify, and some of them you will scourge in your synagogues, and persecute from city to city, so that upon you may fall the guilt of all the righteous blood shed on earth, from the blood of righteous Abel to the blood of Zechariah, the son of Berechiah, whom you murdered between the temple and the altar. Truly I say to you, all these things will come upon this generation."
Matthew 23:33-36

God does not change! He is the same God today that He was 2,000 years ago and the words Jesus spoke to the leaders and judges of Israel regarding the prophets, wise men and scribes of that day have not changed! Our judges and leaders should tremble because of their sins against the Lord! What is the judgment Jesus declared against them?

"You serpents, you brood of vipers, how will you escape the sentence of hell?"

HAVE WE BECOME A NATION OF FOOLS IN THE EYES OF GOD?

> *The fool has said in his heart, "There is no God." They are corrupt; they have committed abominable deeds; There is no one who does good. The LORD has looked down from heaven upon the sons of men to see if there are any who understand, who seek after God. They have all turned aside; together they have become corrupt; There is no one who does good, not even one. Psalm 14:1-3*

The "prophets of Jezebel," operating in our nation have acted corruptly in the eyes of God. As the Psalm declares, they have committed an abominable sin in the eyes of God, and they have become like fools in the eyes of God.

Like "Jezebel," they cannot "cohabitate" with anything that is of God. As the "prophets of Jezebel" they can only cohabitate with the things of Satan that lead our people and our nation away from the worship of God and into the worship idols and the wisdom of man.

Their declaration has gone forth. "There is no God! America does not need God because we have become our *own* gods!"

KNOW THEM BY THEIR FRUIT

In the following scriptures, God uses fruit trees as a "physical example" in order to illustrate a "spiritual truth".

Everyone knows that fruit trees produce fruit. But there are many varieties of fruit trees. You can be *sure* it's an apple tree only if it grows apples. An apple tree never produces bananas. You know exactly what kind of tree it is by the fruit it produces.

"For every tree is known by its own fruit." Luke 6:44

Simple! How can we recognize the false prophets, or bad trees, in our midst? How do you recognize a "prophet of Jezebel?"

Jesus provided the answer, and it has not changed in 2000 years.

> *"Beware of the false prophets, who come to you in sheep's clothing, but inwardly are ravenous wolves. You will know them by their fruits. Grapes are not gathered from thorn bushes, nor figs from thistles, are they? So every good tree bears good fruit, but the bad tree bears bad fruit. A good tree cannot produce bad fruit, nor can a bad tree produce good fruit. Every tree that does not bear good fruit is cut down and thrown into the fire. So then, you will know them by their fruits."* Matthew 7:15-20

A "prophet of Jezebel" produces fruit that will not last. Their fruit is from Satan, it is certainly bad fruit and those who eat it will surely die. Their deeds are the "deeds of the flesh" not of the Spirit of God.

> *Now the deeds of the flesh are evident, which are immorality, impurity, sensuality, idolatry, sorcery, enmities, strife, jealousy, outbursts of anger, disputes, dissensions, factions, envying, drunkenness, carousing, and things like these, of which I forewarn you, just as I have forewarned you, that those who practice such things will not inherit the kingdom of God.* Galatians 5:19-21

By contrast, what kind of fruit is produced by the "prophets of God" through the "Spirit of God"?

> *But the fruit of the Spirit is love, joy, peace, patience, kindness, goodness, faithfulness, gentleness, self-control; against such things there is no law.* Galatians 5:22-23

Notice in these verses it speaks of "fruit of the Spirit" and that it is singular, not plural. Yet, it lists more than one fruit. Why?

Because love is the fruit of the Spirit of God, and out of the love of God in our hearts flows joy, peace, patience, kindness, goodness, faithfulness, gentleness and self-control. Without the love of God, it is impossible for the fruit of the Spirit of God to flow forth from the heart.

Jesus said this of those who bear good fruit.

> *"My Father is glorified by this, that you bear much fruit, and so prove to be My disciples." John 15:8*

WHAT KIND OF FRUIT IS YOUR TREE BEARING?

Ask yourself the question. What kind of fruit is my tree producing?

> *Jesus said, "I am the vine, you are the branches; he who abides in Me and I in him, he bears much fruit, for apart from Me you can do nothing. If anyone does not abide in Me, he is thrown away as a branch and dries up; and they gather them, and cast them into the fire and they are burned. My Father is glorified by this, that you bear much fruit, and so prove to be My disciples." John 15:5-6, 8*

You and I cannot bear good fruit apart from Jesus. Because He is the vine, and we are His branches, we must be connected to the vine or there is no fruit. And His vine can only bear good fruit.

Is your tree producing the fruit from the vine of the Lord, or is your tree producing the fruit of the flesh? Know for certain that the "fruit of the flesh" is never good fruit and one day, just as the Lord prophesied in the following verse, "....*they will be cut down and cast into the fire.*"

Jesus declared in these verses there is living proof if you are a "disciple of God." The proof is that your life will glorify the Father; your life will bear much fruit and thereby prove that you are a disciple of the Living God.

Examine *your* life. Is your life characterized by the "Spirit of God" or by the "deeds of the flesh"? Is the fruit that *your* life is producing good fruit or bad?

CHAPTER 23

THE PROPHETS OF GOD

God does not change, His word does not change, nor does what His prophets teach change!

What the Lord declared to Israel in the Old Testament is as true today as it was a thousand years ago.

> You are My witnesses," declares the LORD, "And My servant whom I have chosen, So that you may know and believe Me And understand that I am He. Before Me there was no God formed, And there will be none after Me. "I, even I, am the LORD, And there is no savior besides Me. "It is I who have declared and saved and proclaimed, And there was no strange god among you; So you are My witnesses," declares the LORD, "And I am God. "Even from eternity I am He, And there is none who can deliver out of My hand; I act and who can reverse it?" Isaiah 43:10-13

The Lord said in these verses, "*Before Me there was no God formed, and there will be none after Me. I, even I, am the Lord, and there is no savior besides Me!*"

Regardless of how many laws the "prophets of Jezebel" pass outlawing God and His Ten Commandments, the Lord has called us as His witnesses to declare to our nation and the world the truth of His word.

"*I am God. Even from Eternity I am He, and there is none who can deliver out of My hand. I act and who can reverse it*"?

The "prophets of Jezebel" that are operating in our nation should tremble before the living God because "*None can deliver them out of God's hand, and from His coming judgment against them. "He acts and who can reverse it!*"

THE PROPHETS OF JEZEBEL DECLARE THE SAME THING THE KORAN DECLARES REGARDING JESUS CHRIST AND THE FATHER

What does the Koran teach regarding the Son of God?

Sura 23:91 "*NEVER DID ALLAH TAKE TO HIMSELF A SON, and never was there with him any (other) god.*"

Sura 17:111 "And say: All praise is due to Allah, *WHO HAS NOT TAKEN A SON* and *WHO HAS NOT A PARTNER in the kingdom.*"

Yet, what does the word of God declare?

> *In the beginning was the Word, and the Word was with God, and the Word was God. He was in the beginning with God. All things came into being by Him, and apart from Him nothing came into being that has come into being. In Him was life, and the life was the light of men. And the Word became flesh, and dwelt among us, and we beheld His glory, glory as of the only begotten from the Father, full of grace and truth. John 1:1-4, 14*

God the Father sent His only Son Jesus Christ and He became flesh and dwelt among men.

CHOOSE THIS DAY WHOM YOU WILL SERVE

Americans are at the same place that the Israelites were when they were challenged by Joshua to choose whom they would serve and whom they would worship.

> *"If it is disagreeable in your sight to serve the LORD, choose for yourselves today whom you will serve: whether the gods which your fathers served which were beyond the River, or the gods of the Amorites in whose land you are living: but as for me and my house, we will serve the LORD." Joshua 24:15*

WHOM WILL YOU CHOOSE TO SERVE AND WORSHIP?

Will you follow the "prophets of Jezebel" in our midst and bow down and worship the wisdom of man that declares, *"There is no Father God, and He did not send His Son to bring remission from sin and eternal life to those who believe in Him?"*

Will you follow those who declare, *"There is no God, therefore His Ten Commandments are meaningless to us, to the children and to the nation?"*

Will you follow the "prophets of Jezebel" who declare, *"The United States and its people have no heritage with God and His Son?"*

Will you follow those who declare, *"There is no God, therefore there is no sin. And where there is no sin there can be no consequences,"* even when the nation's sin is so grievous before Him?

Will you be counted among those like the American Civil Liberties Union who declare, *"Posting the text of The Ten Commandments is not a memorial to a common' secular heritage?"*

Secular heritage? The *heritage* of the United States of America is decidedly *not* secular. The heritage of the United States was founded upon The Ten Commandments and the Bible! Yet, they consistently perpetuate this lie and seek to separate the people from their *true* heritage – The Ten Commandments and the word of God.

Or will you be as Joshua, and choose to serve the One True and Living God?

Your choice will determine the eternal destiny of your soul. The nation's choice will determine its eternal destiny as a nation.

> *"I call heaven and earth to witness against you today, that I have set before you life and death, the blessing and the curse. So choose life in order that you may live, you and your descendants." Deuteronomy 30:19*

This book is written so that ALL may choose life!

TEST THE SPIRIT AND KNOW THE KINGDOM

America is a nation filled with deception put forth by the "Prophets of Jezebel." So how do we know if something is from the Kingdom of God or from the kingdom of Satan?

The test is a simple one. Does the law or action taken lead us toward God and into the obedience of His commandments or away from them? Does the law or action taken lead us to worship God or to worship Satan and the things of Satan?

Jesus said it clearly.

> *"He who is not with Me is against Me; and he who does not gather with Me, scatters"* Luke 11:23

The "spirit of the anti-Christ," operating through the "prophets of Jezebel," has led the nation away from God and away from His commandments to worship the commandments and the wisdom of man.

TEST THE SPIRIT

> *Beloved, do not believe every spirit, but test the spirits to see whether they are from God, because many false prophets have gone out into the world. By this you know the Spirit of God: every spirit that confesses that Jesus Christ has come in the flesh is from God; and every spirit that does not confess Jesus is not from God; this is the spirit of the antichrist, of which you have heard that it is coming, and now it is already in the world. I John 4:1-3*

Always test the spirit, to see whether they are from God or from Satan.

Each of us who have been blessed by God with children must decide if we will follow His commandments, teach them to our children and lead them to the Kingdom of God, or turn away from God and teach them to follow the commandments and wisdom of man into the kingdom of Satan!

We are to give life to our children, grandchildren and friends. Teach them to test the spirits, to fear God and choose the way of the Lord.

> *Who is the man who fears the LORD? He will instruct him in the way he should choose. His soul will abide in prosperity, And his descendants will inherit the land. The secret of the LORD is for those who fear Him, And He will make them know His covenant. Psalm 25:12-14*

CHAPTER 24

THE SHEDDING OF INNOCENT BLOOD

It is interesting to note that shortly after prayer and The Ten Commandments were effectively eliminated from America's schools, the "shedding of innocent blood" became an acceptable practice in the nation as well.

The modern day "prophets of Jezebel" again seduced and influenced nation's court system to make it legal for a woman to sacrifice her unborn child through abortion under the banner of "Women's Rights."

Again we see that we do know them by their fruit, and these modern day "prophets of Jezebel" seek to change times and laws that are in *direct opposition* to the commandments of God. In the Bible, the word of God, the Lord declares that He *hates* the "shedding of innocent blood."

> *There are six things which the LORD hates, yes, seven which are an abomination to Him: Haughty eyes, a lying tongue, And hands that shed innocent blood, A heart that devises wicked plans, Feet that run rapidly to evil, A false witness who utters lies, And one who spreads strife among brothers. Proverbs 6:16-19*

The "spirit of the anti-Christ" has deceived America into believing, promoting, legalizing and teaching that abortion and shedding innocent blood is an acceptable practice and has given it the name, "Choice."

But the Lord declared in these verses, "I hate hands that shed innocent blood!"

When the children of Israel came to conquer the lands of their inheritance, often they were commanded by God to destroy all the inhabitants of that land, every man, woman and child. Why would a loving God issue such a harsh command?

These nations that Israel was to conquer were wicked and perverse, and much of the worship of their foreign gods involved deviant sexual practices. As a result, the people, men, women and children, were riddled with diseased bodies and minds. God did not want His children to adopt their gods, customs and practices *because* He loved them and wanted them spared from the wickedness and disease that had permeated these corrupt nations.

One of their more horrific worship practices was to take the unwanted children that resulted from their previous "acts of worship" and burn them alive on the altar to Molech, their god of pleasure. And God *hated* this shedding of innocent blood.

But, sadly the children of Israel did not fully obey the Lord's command. And, over the years, just as God had warned, their leaders and then their people began to fall prey to temptation and chose to follow these evil and ungodly practices and to participate in their abominations before God.

Just as the "prophets of Jezebel" led the northern Kingdom of Israel to sacrifice their children to a foreign god, Americans have also been led to sacrifice their unborn children to a foreign god. America has become a nation like the northern Kingdom of Israel and, in the practices of worship to the god of pleasure people are sacrificing their unborn children to the gods of lust, passion and indifference.

GOD SEVERELY JUDGED ISRAEL WHEN THEY SACRIFICED TO A FOREIGN GOD BY SHEDDING INNOCENT BLOOD

> *Then they made their sons and their daughter's pass through the fire, and practiced divination and enchantments, and sold themselves to do evil in the sight of the LORD, provoking Him. So the LORD was very angry with Israel and removed them from His sight; none was left except the tribe of Judah. II Kings 17:17-18*

This was no insignificant judgment! God severely judged the northern kingdom of Israel for their sin. He brought forth the Assyrian army and allowed them to not only conquer the entire northern Kingdom of Israel, but to forcibly remove the entire Jewish population from the northern kingdom, never again to return!

Only the southern Kingdom of Judah, which included the tribe of Benjamin, now remained in the land to inherit the blessings of God.

In America, more than 4,000 innocent babies are aborted each and every day. The saline solutions that are inserted into the woman's uterus have the effect of burning the baby alive in their mother's womb. Is America any different than those nations of old that burned their babies alive as a sacrifice to *their* god of pleasure? Is America any different than the northern Kingdom of Israel?

Sin is sin, whether it is a nation or a person, and although some may believe we are exempt from God's judgment, we are not. We need only to look at Israel's punishment to realize that the time for the United States to be judged is coming if the people do not repent.

God does not change. He is the same yesterday, today, and tomorrow!

> *"Moreover, you took your sons and daughters whom you had borne to Me and sacrificed them to idols to be devoured. Were your harlotries so small a matter? You slaughtered My children and offered them up to idols by causing them to pass through the fire." Ezekiel 16:20-21*

God is asking America the same question He asked Israel. "Were your harlotries so small a matter?"

Abortion and the shedding of innocent blood is no small matter in the eyes of the Lord. America has caused her children to be slaughtered. What America has done is no small matter with God!

Abortion is an act that often seeks to cover up or hide the sin of fornication, which is sexual intercourse outside of marriage. This is a sin against God, and one that He hates.

At the heart of God is the desire to give and to forgive us our sins. This redemptive process is true. I know it is true not only because the Bible says it is, but because I am a living testimony of the effect His forgiveness has had on my life and in the lives of countless others.

Confession and forgiveness go to the very heart of God. It is why He sent His Son to die on the cross for our sins. Confession and forgiveness result in transformation of the soul and spirit from sin, bondage and darkness to forgiveness, freedom and light.

When we humble ourselves before God, our soul comes under the gaze of His loving eyes. In His holy presence our hearts are pierced to the quick and we are ready for the Lord to change us. Only through honest confession before the Lord is it possible to have the chains of guilt, the bondage of sin and the power of the evil one shattered so completely that they can never oppress you again.

This experience of confession puts us squarely "in God's sight" where He can deal with and forgive our confessed sins. We must place ourselves on the altar of God as a living sacrifice, so that the precious blood of Jesus can remove our sins.

It is upon the altar of God, and in His loving and holy presence, that we learn who we are and who God is. It is upon the altar and at the foot of the cross of Jesus Christ that we find salvation, forgiveness and freedom.

> *If we confess our sins, He is faithful and righteous to forgive us our sins and to cleanse us from all unrighteousness. If we say that we have not sinned, we make Him a liar and His word is not in us. I John 1:9-10*

There is not one person reading this book who has not sinned. Perhaps you have been guilty of the sin of abortion, or of causing someone to have an abortion. Perhaps you have committed the sin of adultery. Or perhaps you have been guilty of not knowing or teaching your children the word of God and His Ten Commandments. Perhaps you have never walked with God, and you have been following the precepts and teaching of man and the "prophets of Jezebel."

You can live with your sin, and as the verses above declare you can say, "I have not sinned." However, Jesus said that when you say this, you "make Him a liar and His word is not in you."

We all have to make choices in life. It is a fact that it is extremely difficult for many to bare their soul before the Lord, to get down on their knees and confess their sins before Him.

We can live in bondage to guilt, sin and Satan, or we can know the freedom that comes to those who walk with Christ. The choice is each one of ours to make.

Truth is truth. Abortion and the shedding of innocent blood is a sin before God and America is a land stained with the blood of millions of innocent children! Regardless of what the court system says, regardless of what those who advocate "Women's Rights" declare, the Lord God is the Creator of all things, and He loves His creation.

> *For You formed my inward parts; You wove me in my mother's womb. I will give thanks to You, for I am fearfully and wonderfully made; Wonderful are Your works, And my soul knows it very well. My frame was not hidden from You, When I was made in secret, And skillfully wrought in the depths of the earth; Your eyes have seen my unformed substance; And in Your book were all written The days that were ordained for me, When as yet there was not one of them. Psalm 139:13-16*

Children are a gift from God. It is God who "fearfully and wonderfully" formed us in our mother's womb. And each and every child born and *unborn* is precious in His sight.

> *Behold, children are a gift of the Lord; the fruit of the womb is a reward. Psalm 127:3*

ABORTION STIFLES CREATION

It is a medical fact that the greater the number of abortions a woman has, the less likely she will be able to bring forth life. Abortion brings death to the womb, just as it brings death to the unborn child.

The "prophets of Jezebel" in the nation's midst want to abort the prayers, abort the children, abort God's word, abort His Ten Commandments and ultimately abort America as a nation under God.

We are being called by God to choose whom we will serve and worship! The Apostle Paul exhorted us to,

> ... *work out your salvation with fear and trembling; for it is God who is at work in you, both to will and to work for His good pleasure. Philippians 2:12-13*

We are called to understand that our salvation is both an event and a process of walking with God each and every day of our lives. We are all being called to oppose those who are seeking to "abort our children, abort our prayers, abort God's Word, abort His Ten Commandments and abort the nation."

There is no middle ground. There is a remnant in the nation who is willing to stand against the "prophets of Jezebel." They are the modern day Elijah's.

Where do you stand? Are you an Elijah, or a "prophet of Jezebel?" Will you be like Moses, and intercede for America and Israel and for your family? Will you dare to stand with the Lord against the "prophets of Jezebel?"

> *But as for you, stand here by Me, that I may speak to you all the commandments and the statutes and the judgments which you shall teach them, that they may observe them in the land which I give them to possess. So you shall observe to do just as the LORD your God has commanded you; you shall not turn aside to the right or to the left. You shall walk in all the way which the LORD your God has commanded you, that you may live and that it may be well with you, and that you may prolong your days in the land which you will possess.*
> *Deuteronomy 5:31-33*

CHAPTER 25

A GODLY MAN IN AN UNGODLY SOCIETY

Jesus commanded us to recognize the "signs of the times." What are the "signs of the times" that we are to recognize? We are to recognize that we are living in an ungodly society where immorality prevails and where the "prophets of Jezebel" rule and reign.

To recognize the signs of the times is one thing, but how do we go about living our daily lives in the midst of such a society? How do we raise godly children and maintain godly marriages in such a society?

Where should we look for examples so that we can learn how to live godly lives in an ungodly society? The best examples are found in the Bible.

One of the greatest examples of a man who lived a godly life in the midst of an ungodly society is found in the life of the prophet Daniel.

As we examine the early life of Daniel, we find him at the tender age of fourteen living in the Kingdom of Babylon. How did Daniel, a Hebrew who was born in Jerusalem come to be living in the midst of an ungodly nation like Babylon?

Daniel was taken as a slave when the southern Kingdom of Judah, where he lived, fell into the hands of Nebuchadnezzar, King of Babylon. How did it come about that Judah was given into the hands of an ungodly king?

DISOBEDIENCE TO GOD'S COMMANDS BROUGHT GOD'S JUDGMENT ON ISRAEL

Because of Israel's disobedience to obey God's command "to give the land a Sabbath rest every seven years," the Lord gave Judah, the southern Kingdom of Israel, into the hands of King Nebuchadnezzar of Babylon.

In the third year of the reign of Jehoiakim king of Judah, Nebuchadnezzar king of Babylon came to Jerusalem and besieged it. The Lord gave Jehoiakim, king of Judah, into his hand along with some of the vessels of the house of God; and he brought them to the land of Shinar, to the house of his god, and he brought the vessels into the treasury of his god. Daniel 1:1-2

In these verses we learn that disobedience to God's commands brought judgment upon the southern Kingdom of Israel, known as Judah.

We see that it was the Lord, not man, who gave Jehoiakim, King of Judah into the hands of the King of Babylon along with the vessels of the Temple of God in Jerusalem.

It was God's hand of judgment against Judah that caused them to be completely removed from the land of Israel for seventy years!

Daniel was taken captive as a slave to Babylon when he was just a youth of 14 years old. His parents were killed in the siege and he, along with all the other captives from Judah, was forced to walk the 1,500 miles to Babylon in chains.

Yet, the hand of the Lord was on Daniel from his birth because the Lord knew Daniel's heart for Him.

Then the king ordered Ashpenaz, the chief of his officials, to bring in some of the sons of Israel, including some of the royal family and of the nobles, youths in whom was no defect, who were good-looking, showing intelligence in every branch of wisdom, endowed with understanding and discerning knowledge, and who had ability for serving in the king's court; and he ordered him to teach them the literature and language of the Chaldeans. The king appointed for them a daily ration from the king's choice food and from the wine which he drank, and appointed that they should be educated three years, at the end of which they were to enter the king's personal service. Daniel 1:3-5

We see in these verses that, by the merciful hand of the Lord, Daniel was one of the youths selected by Ashpenaz to go into the king's service. We also learn a great deal about the physical and mental characteristics that the Lord had bestowed upon Daniel.

"He was good looking, showing intelligence in every branch of wisdom, endowed with understanding and discerning knowledge, and who had ability for the king's court."

Think about *that* for a moment! How many fourteen year-old children do you personally know that you could describe in this manner? Undoubtedly, they are few and far between! Why are there so few fourteen year-old children today whom we could attest have the physical and mental characteristics of a Daniel? As we will learn, it had a great deal to do with Daniel's parents. It was in their heart to teach him the precepts of God so that Daniel would choose to follow God no matter what the circumstances.

We learn that Daniel, along with the other youths selected for the king's court, were given a daily food ration, and that they were each instructed in the language, customs and literature of the Babylonians for three years.

But why did the king order Daniel and the youths to be trained in the language, customs and literature of the Babylonians?

Daniel was a Hebrew who was taught from his youth the great Hebrew Shemah of Deuteronomy 6.

> *"Hear O Israel, the Lord our God, the Lord is one!"*
> *Deuteronomy 6:4*

Daniel was taught from birth there is only one God, the God of Israel! There is no other God!

The Babylonians worshiped many pagan gods and bowed down to idols. The literature, language and customs of the Babylonians were steeped in the worship of demons, idols, witchcraft, sorcery and godlessness.

The king wanted to transform Daniel and all the Hebrew youths, from worshiping the living God to becoming as the Babylonians who worshiped idols and many gods. The king wanted them to be conformed to the world over which he ruled. Babylon was a kingdom that did not know the living God.

> *You adulteresses, do you not know that friendship with the world is hostility toward God? Therefore whoever wishes to be a friend of the world makes himself an enemy of God. James 4:4*

Do you see any similarity between the time of Daniel and today? Are not the "prophets of Jezebel" operating in our nation the same way, seeking to lead our children away from the living God, to worship the culture, customs and wisdom of man?

Satan has not changed, nor have his ways and methods changed. His goal is the same today as it was in Daniel's day. Satan wants to lead our children away from our God to bow down and worship *him.* Satan wants to destroy our marriages and our families by leading many into adultery and sin.

Satan wants us to worship and bow down to everything that is hostile toward God! Satan wants us to have friendship with the corrupt things of the world so we will join him in becoming enemies of God.

The king wanted to transform Daniel from a Hebrew into a Babylonian, a worshiper of the true and living God to the worshiper of idols. The king wanted to transform Daniel from following what is holy to following that which is unholy.

We see in the next verses that the king even changed Daniels name. The name Daniel in Hebrew means, "God is my judge!"

> *Then the commander of the officials assigned new names to them; and to Daniel he assigned the name Belteshazzar." Daniel 1:7*

The name Belteshazzar means, "Whom Baal favors." The commander sought to change Daniel's name from the holy to the unholy. The commander sought to change Daniel to one who follows a pagan god named Baal rather than one who follows the God who was his judge.

HOW DID DANIEL RESPOND TO ALL THIS?

But Daniel purposed in his heart that he would not defile himself with the king's choice food or with the wine which he drank; so he sought permission from the commander of the officials that he might not defile himself. Daniel 1:8

Why is it that Daniel did not object to having his name changed, or to learning the language, customs and literature of the Babylonians, but refused to defile himself with the king's choice food? Daniel refused to eat the king's choice food because it had been "sacrificed to idols."

Why did Daniel refuse to eat food sacrificed to idols?

Daniel's parents had taught him from birth the Levitical laws regarding eating things that are "Unclean before the Lord." But were these Levitical laws put in place by God just for health reasons? We find the answer to this question in Leviticus, Chapter 11.

"I AM THE LORD YOUR GOD, CONSECRATE YOURSELVES AND BE HOLY, FOR I AM HOLY."
Leviticus 11:44

God is Holy, and Daniel purposed in his heart to always be holy before his God. By refusing to eat the king's choice food, Daniel was putting his life on the line. He was a slave, and slaves do not dispute their master's commands. Yet, Daniel chose to follow God's ways, not man's ways.

DANIEL PURPOSED IN HIS HEART

The key to understanding the character of Daniel is in the verse where we read, *"He purposed in his heart not to defile himself with the king's food or wine!"* What does it mean "to purpose in your heart"?

200

To purpose in your heart means to make up your mind *before* the test comes exactly what you will do, so that *when* the testing comes the decision has already been made.

That is *exactly* what Daniel did. He made his mind up *before* the test came, so that *when* it came there was no decision to make. Daniel chose to follow God and to be holy, because God is Holy!

WHAT HELPED DANIEL TO FOLLOW GOD INSTEAD OF MAN?

Daniel chose to follow God and not man because that is what his parents taught him to do from birth. Daniel's parents believed the word of the Lord and taught it to him from birth.

> *"Hear, O Israel! The LORD is our God, the LORD is one! You shall love the LORD your God with all your heart and with all your soul and with all your might. These words, which I am commanding you today, shall be on your heart. You shall teach them diligently to your sons and shall talk of them when you sit in your house and when you walk by the way and when you lie down and when you rise up." Deuteronomy 6:4-7*

Daniel's parents believed the word of God! They obeyed the word of God and diligently taught the word of God to Daniel from his youth.

WHAT YOU TEACH OR DO NOT TEACH YOUR CHILDREN MATTERS

The "prophets of Jezebel" operating in American society today are not any different from the King of Babylon, or from Queen Jezebel in during the time of Elijah. They all have the same goal.

As we have written before, the "prophets of Jezebel" operating in the American society have essentially removed prayer to God from the schools and the teaching of His Ten Commandments to the children; they seek to lead the children away from worshiping the living God, to believing there is no God; they seek to cause the women to sacrifice their children through abortion to the idols of lust, sex and indifference.

Daniel's parents *taught* him to purpose in his heart to love the Lord with all his heart, his mind, his strength and soul!

Daniel's Parents taught him!

Always obey God's commandments!
Always believe in God's power of deliverance!
Always believe God's promises!
Never to bow down to other gods or idols!
Pray to God before making a decision!
Seek the Wisdom of God, not man!
Never be conformed to the world and follow the ungodly ways of the people around him!
Don't look at the circumstances; always stay focused on God and His promises!
To purpose in his heart to always follow God, not man!
Always fear God, not man!

WHAT ARE YOU TEACHING YOUR CHILDREN?

Are you teaching your children and grandchildren to purpose in their hearts to love the Lord with all their hearts, minds, strength and souls? Is your life a living example of a parent who chooses to follow God instead of man? Are you a living example of a godly husband to your wife or a godly wife to your husband? Do you pray together as a family? Do you read and study God's word and teach it diligently to your children? Who do you fear, man or God?

Who do you follow, God or the "prophets of Jezebel"? Whom do your children follow?

WHAT WILL THE CHILDREN DO WHEN THE TIME OF TESTING COMES UPON THEM?

Ask yourself, what will your children do when a time of testing comes upon them and you are not there to protect them?

Ask yourself, what will they do when the time of testing comes upon them and they do not believe in the armor and power of God?

Have you, like Daniel, purposed in your heart what you will do before the testing comes upon you? Have you taught your children to purpose in their hearts what they will do when their testing comes upon them? If *you* have not, how do you expect your *children* to?

When your children are offered drugs or alcohol, what will they choose to do?
When your children are alone on a date and the issue is to have sex or abstain, what will they choose?
When your children must decide to follow the ways of God or the ways of Satan whom will they choose?
How about you? When Satan tempts you with adultery, drugs, alcohol, pornography or deception at your workplace, have you purposed in your heart to resist him before the test comes upon you?

Ask yourself the question, when the time of testing comes for my children what will they do? Know for certain that if you have not taught your children to "purpose in their hearts" to obey God in what they will do, they will almost certainly fall prey to the schemes of the evil one who is seeking to destroy their very soul.

When your time of testing comes, it is not what you say, but what you do that reveals what you believe about God. What are you teaching your children and grandchildren about what you really believe?

The Apostle Paul instructed us in the book of II Corinthians to test ourselves.

> *Test yourselves to see if you are in the faith; examine yourselves! Or do you not recognize this about yourselves, that Jesus Christ is in you unless indeed you fail the test? But I trust that you will realize that we ourselves do not fail the test. II Corinthians 13:5-6*

In the Bible, the book of Daniel reveals that throughout his life, Daniel was an exemplary of a man who honored and obeyed God. No matter what the circumstance, danger or difficulty Daniel from his youth and to his dying day as an old man honored and respected by friend and foe alike, purposed in his heart to walk in the ways of the Lord.

Are you seeking to live a godly life in an ungodly society? Are you teaching your children and grandchildren to live a godly life? You can choose to be a Daniel. You can teach them to be a Daniel. The nation, the families, the churches and synagogues desperately need Daniels!

Will you dare to be a Daniel?

CHAPTER 26

GHOSTS FROM THE PAST

We have labored diligently to make the point that the "prophets of Jezebel" in our society have one specific purpose. To cause our nation, our leaders and our people to turn away from following God, His word and His commandments and instead bow down and worship the things of Satan.

In our nation's schools our children are being taught there is no creator, therefore there is no God. Our children are being taught that they evolved from monkeys and are being led away from following Him and His commandments. When a nation or a people turn away from God they become enemies of God and enemies of the people of God.

There are many God fearing people in America, but their numbers are diminishing. They are constantly coming under attack in the media, the movies and at work, as being bigoted, unenlightened, narrow minded, conservative and prejudiced.

As the spirit of the anti-Christ grows stronger, it will polarize those who oppose God and they will avidly seek to destroy all those who follow God and His word. This spirit quickly changes from the spirit of opposition into the spirit of hatred, and this age-old hatred, when it rears its ugly head, always turns against the Jews and in the last days it will turn against born-again Christians.

This spirit of anti-Semitism (hatred of Jews) is alive and well today in many nations. The spirit of anti-Semitism has once again arisen in Europe and England just as it did in the days of Hitler. The ghost from the past has sprung to life once again.

At the beginning of 2002, the Deputy Foreign Minister of France, Michael Melchior declared, "France is the worst western country for the number of cases of aggression and anti-Semitic incidents. We sense the hesitation on the part of the authorities to take the necessary steps to stop this."

In France, during the year 2001, there were 320 anti-Jewish incidents. Almost one a day, including the October burning of the Trappes synagogue, the first Jewish house of worship destroyed in France since World War II. Today, the 600,000 Jews living in France are experiencing daily acts of violence against them and their Jewish institutions, while the government of France is doing little or nothing to stop it.

Much of the hatred is fueled by French media coverage that is so one sided against Israel and the Jews that it can only be termed "managed propaganda against Israel and the Jews." France's five million-strong Islamic immigrant community is treated nightly to horrible scenes of burned Palestinian bodies and wailing mothers. Little is ever shown of the suicide bombers that have killed and maimed thousands of Israelis.

Even France's foreign minister got into the act recently when he let his guard down at a dinner party, while in England, and called Israel, quote, *"that shitty little country."*

Europe's growing Muslim population is working daily to fan the flames of hatred against Jews and against Israel. Germany is home to extremist Islamic terrorists as evidenced by the fact that several of the September 11th terrorists lived and trained there.

On April 15th 2002, Arabs attacked a mother and her daughter in the underground train in Berlin, Germany. They approached the woman after noticing the daughter was wearing a necklace with a Star of David on it, around her neck. They asked her if she was Jewish and when she replied she was, they hit her in the face and ripped the necklace off of her. When her mother tried to defend her she was beaten severely. None of the other passengers on the train did anything to intervene.

In the same month a Jewish mother and her adult daughter were punched in the face on a Berlin subway car and two twenty-one year old American Jews were attacked while walking along one of Berlin's major streets after visiting a synagogue in the area.

Incidents like this are taking place in Belgium, France, Norway and many other European countries. The news media in Europe and England have become hostile toward Israel and the Jewish people as well.

One of England's noted poets, Tom Paulin of Oxford University, was quoted in the Egyptian daily *Al-Ahram* recently as saying, "All the Jewish settlers should be shot dead. I think they are Nazi racists. I feel nothing but hatred for them." For good measure he added what most of Europe, England and the Arab nations feel today, "I never believed that Israel had the right to exist at all."

In this statement we have the heart of the matter. "I never believed that Israel had the right to exist at all!" In this one sentence are embodied the words of Satan's himself. *"Israel should never exist at all."*

Do you remember what was written in the Psalms regarding the enemies of Israel in the last days?

> *O GOD, do not remain quiet; Do not be silent and, O God, do not be still. For behold, Your enemies make an uproar, And those who hate You have exalted themselves. They make shrewd plans against Your people, And conspire together against Your treasured ones. They have said, "Come, and let us wipe them out as a nation, That the name of Israel be remembered no more." For they have conspired together with one mind; Against You they make a covenant: Psalm 83:1-5*

The words of this Psalm, written thousands of years ago, prophesied the day would come when Israel would be a nation once again. This prophecy declares the Arab Nations and their allies would conspire together for one purpose. They have said, *"Come, and let us wipe them out as a nation, that the name of Israel be remembered no more."*

Just as the Lord declared, the spirit of the anti-Christ has arisen in these last days to destroy Israel and the Jews. There is an important lesson in these verses for all of those who have risen to destroy Israel.

These verses say that they have not only risen against Israel and the Jews, but also against the God of Israel. The verses say, *"For they have conspired together with one mind; Against You they make a covenant."*

When nations or people come against Israel and the Jews, they must understand that they are coming against the God of the Jews, the God of Israel.

> *"But you, Israel, My servant, Jacob whom I have chosen, Descendant of Abraham My friend, You whom I have taken from the ends of the earth, and called from its remotest parts And said to you, 'You are My servant, I have chosen you and not rejected you. 'Do not fear, for I am with you; Do not anxiously look about you, for I am your God. I will strengthen you, surely I will help you, Surely I will uphold you with My righteous right hand.'"*
> *Isaiah 41:8-10*

To those who declare war against Israel and seek her destruction, the Lord has a word for you on this matter.

> *"Behold, all those who are angered at you will be shamed and dishonored; Those who contend with you will be as nothing and will perish. You will seek those who quarrel with you, but will not find them, Those who war with you will be as nothing and non-existent. For I am the LORD your God, who upholds your right hand, Who says to you, 'Do not fear, I will help you."* *Isaiah 41:11-13*

These are not idle words written in some obscure book. These words are written in the Bible and come from the heart and mind of God. Few believe these words, but the day is fast approaching when the nations and the people of the earth will know the truth of these words. For thus says the Lord God of Israel, *"Those who contend with you and make war with you will be as nothing and will perish. Those who make war with you will be as nothing and non-existent."*

Why is all of this so important to America? It is important because the day is coming when America will turn against Israel and the Jews, just as their European counterparts have.

"Behold, I am going to make Jerusalem a cup that causes reeling to all the peoples around; and when the siege is against Jerusalem, it will also be against Judah. And it will come about in that day that I will make Jerusalem a heavy stone for all the peoples; and all who lift it will be severely injured. And all the nations of the earth will be gathered against it." Zechariah 12:2-3

Notice the last verse of this prophecy says, "and all the nations of the earth will be gathered against it." All means all, including America.

When this day comes, and it will, they will also turn against the born-again Christians in America. Impossible you say? The day is approaching when the anti-Christ will arise and demand all who dwell upon the earth do one specific thing.

All who dwell on the earth will worship him, everyone whose name has not been written from the foundation of the world in the book of life of the Lamb who has been slain. And it was given to him to give breath to the image of the beast, so that the image of the beast, (the anti-Christ) would even speak and cause as many as do not worship the image of the beast to be killed. Revelation 13:8, 15

Twice in these verses in Revelation, it says that all those who do not bow down and *"worship the image of the beast will be killed."* The only ones who will not bow down and worship the image of the beast are those whose names have been written in the book of life of the Lamb of God.

During World War II, the Jews of Europe were herded into Hitler's concentration camps and exterminated while most of the Christian world looked on and did nothing. Many Christians today still believe that the persecution of the Jews and Israel in modern times really has nothing to do with them personally. They are wrong. It has everything to do with them, their families, their lives and their eternal destiny.

The verses in Revelation reveal that the anti-Christ is coming, and when he comes he will demand one thing of every human being living on the earth, that "*all who dwell on the earth worship him.*" All means all. No exceptions.

If you are a Jew this means you cannot worship the God of Abraham, Isaac and Jacob. You must bow down and worship the anti-Christ or die.

If you are a Christian, this means you cannot worship Jesus Christ, the Son of God. You must bow down and worship the anti-Christ or die. There is no middle ground with the anti-Christ. Worship him or die.

What will you do if you are a Christian and you are not "raptured" when you thought you were going to be "raptured"? What will you do if you are called upon to be like your Lord and Savior Jesus Christ and endure suffering?

What if you must face what Peter, Paul, John and James faced? What if you come face to face with the same persecution that our brothers and sisters in the Sudan, Indonesia, Pakistan and other Muslim nations have gone through and are still facing?

Will you choose to bow down and worship a foreign god, or will you choose to perish for your Lord and Savior Jesus Christ? This time the Christians and the Jews are going to be in the same boat. And the reason is obvious.

The God of Abraham, Isaac, and Jacob and His Son Jesus Christ are the same God!

In these last days it is impossible to attack one and not attack the other. They are one and the same God, just as Jesus said.

> *"The glory which You have given Me I have given to them, that they may be one, just as We are one." John 17:22*

Many Christians who believe in a "pre-tribulation rapture" are absolutely certain they will never experience any tribulation, and will be *"raptured"* before the persecution comes.

I ask you, did Jesus suffer? Did Peter, John, James and the other disciples suffer? Are you greater than them?

In Jesus' last message to the churches in Revelation, we find the same admonition in every instance where He addresses the churches and their members.

To the angel of the church in Ephesus write,

> *"He who has an ear let him hear what the Spirit says to the churches. To him who overcomes, I will grant to eat of the tree of life which is in the Paradise of God."*
> *Revelation 2:7*

To the angel of the church in Smyrna write,

> *"He who has an ear let him hear what the Spirit says to the churches. He who overcomes will not be hurt by the second death." Revelation 2:11*

To the angel of the church of Pergamum write,

> *"He who has an ear, let him hear what the Spirit says to the churches. To him who overcomes, to him I will give some of the hidden manna, and I will give him a white stone, and a new name written on the stone which no one knows but he who receives it." Revelation 2:17*

To the angel of the church in Thyatira write,

> *"He who overcomes, and he who keeps My deeds until the end, to him I will give authority over the nations; and he shall rule them with a rod of iron, as the vessels of the potter are broken to pieces, as I also have received authority from My Father; and I will give him the morning star. He who has an ear let him hear what the Spirit says to the churches." Revelation 2:26-29*

211

To the angel of the church of Sardis write,

> "He who overcomes will thus be clothed in white garments; and I will not erase his name from the book of life, and I will confess his name before My Father and before His angels. He who has an ear let him hear what the Spirit says to the churches." Revelation 3:5-6

To the angel of the church in Philadelphia write,

> "He who overcomes, I will make him a pillar in the temple of My God, and he will not go out from it anymore; and I will write on him the name of My God, and the name of the city of My God, the new Jerusalem, which comes down out of heaven from My God, and My new name. He who has an ear let him hear what the Spirit says to the churches." Revelation 3:12-13

To the angel of the church in Laodicea write,

> "He who overcomes, I will grant to him to sit down with Me on My throne, as I also overcame and sat down with My Father on His throne. He who has an ear let him hear what the Spirit says to the churches." Revelation 3:21-22

Could it possibly be that since we are not greater than our Lord and Savior that we *are* going to have to suffer some tribulation before the Lord returns?

Why did Jesus in every instance choose to single out those in the church whom He knew would overcome, and what exactly are they going to have to "overcome"?

I believe that some are going to have to "overcome" a part of the tribulation that is beginning to manifest itself upon the earth. Believe it or not, just like the Jews, the believing Christians are going to "experience some tribulation." However, Jesus said He would keep some from the hour of testing because they persevered by keeping His word.

"Because you have kept the word of My perseverance, I also will keep you from the hour of testing, that hour which is about to come upon the whole world, to test those who dwell on the earth." Revelation 3:10

Will you be one of the ones whom He will keep from the hour of testing?

Many Christians will take issue with this, because to consider experiencing any form of tribulation is not something they want to even contemplate. Jesus commands us to remember because they persecuted Him they will also persecute those who follow Him.

"Remember the word that I said to you, 'A slave is not greater than his master.' If they persecuted Me, they will also persecute you; if they kept My word, they will keep yours also." John 15:20

In these verses Jesus is addressing, *"To him who overcomes."* Jesus said it plainly, *"A slave is not greater than his master, and if they persecuted Me, they will also persecute you."*

These words were not just meant for the disciples and first century Christians.

But notice, in every case after Jesus addressed *"To him who overcomes"* came the amazing and wonderful promises, *"I will give, I will grant, I will make!"* Jesus promises great and eternal rewards *"to Him who overcomes"* the coming persecution.

In the twenty-first Chapter of Revelation, the Apostle Paul describes a revelation given to him by God of a new heaven and a new earth; of the glorious and holy new Jerusalem where God dwells in the midst thereof and where there are no more tears, no more pain and no more death. And Paul, inspired by God writes,

"He who overcomes shall inherit these things, and I will be his God and he will be My son." Revelation 21:7

Will you be *"One who overcomes?"*

CHAPTER 27

THE PLAN OF HAMAN OR THE PLAN OF GOD

The world today is faced with an enigma. How does the world solve the continuing problems in the Middle East? There are problems between Israel, the Arab nations and the Palestinians as well as problems between America, Iraq and Iran.

Iraq, Iran and Syria are terrorist Islamic nations who sponsor terrorism throughout the world. There seems to be no rational solution to dealing with these nations.

The Israeli – Palestinian problem defies human solution because the foundational causes are spiritual. Arafat and the Arab nations do not want peace and they have never wanted peace. What they want is to destroy Israel.

When you watch the news about Israel on TV you are usually seeing events as they happen and the editorial comments by CNN, BBC, NBC, CBS, ABC and FOX News. All reflect the viewpoint of man, not God.

Today in the media there is absolutely no biblical perspective coming forth from any source. Presidents, Prime Ministers, Foreign Ministers, Kings and Secretaries of State, all reflect the wisdom of man, *never* God, where Israel is concerned.

So, what is coming in the months ahead? What plan will the nations hatch to destroy Israel? On Passover Eve of 2002, the world was introduced to the plan that will soon be proposed to bring about the destruction of Israel - the Saudi Peace Proposal.

Without any biblical perspective, many governments acclaimed it as "amazing" since it came forth from the seat of Islam. Remember, this Saudi Peace Plan came from the same nation that spawned Bin Laden and fifteen of the nineteen terrorists who flew airplanes into the Twin Towers of New York City and the Pentagon on September 11, 2001.

214

So, with that as a reminder, let's examine this "so called" peace plan from a biblical perspective. Perhaps it will shed some light on the coming situation from God's perspective, rather than from a human perspective.

THE PLAN OF HAMAN

In the Bible, the book of Esther tells the story of a plot by a man named Haman, who wanted to completely annihilate all the Jews living in the kingdom of the Medes and Persians.

Haman became so angry with Mordecai, a Jew who would not bow down to him, that he hatched a plot to exterminate all the Jews in the kingdom. Haman went to the king and offered money to him to allow him to carry out his extermination plot.

> *"If it is pleasing to the king, let it be decreed that they, (The Jews) be destroyed, and I will pay ten thousand talents of silver into the hands of those who carry on the king's business, to put into the king's treasuries." Then the king took his signet ring from his hand and gave it to Haman, the son of Hammedatha the Agagite, the enemy of the Jews. Esther 3:9-10*

In these short verses we see that the "plan of Haman" was the same as the "plan of Hitler" and it is the same plan that is being hatched today.

Haman believed that since the king had given the Jews into his hands, their destruction was assured!

Haman believed the Jews were now destined for annihilation because what power on earth could possibly defy the kings proclamation?

What Haman did not know or understand was that the Jews have been and always will be in the hands of the God of Israel, not man!

Yet, Haman could not act until the king issued the formal written decree and sealed it with his signet ring.

Then the king's scribes were summoned on the thirteenth day of the first month, and it was written just as Haman commanded to the king's satraps, to the governors who were over each province and to the princes of each people, each province according to its script, each people according to its language, being written in the name of King Ahasuerus and sealed with the king's signet ring. Letters were sent by couriers to all the king's provinces to destroy, to kill and to annihilate all the Jews, both young and old, women and children, in one day, the thirteenth day of the twelfth month, which is the month Adar, and to seize their possessions as plunder. Esther 3:12-13

One of the most significant things in these verses is the date that the decree was issued. It was issued on the thirteenth day of the first month.

What is so significant about this date? The thirteenth day of the first Jewish month is Passover Seder Eve!

It is the exact night the Lord commanded all Israel to celebrate the Passover as an everlasting memorial in order to recount their deliverance from Egypt to their children.

The plot of Haman to exterminate the Jews was decreed on Passover eve. So, what in the world does this have to do with events taking place in the Middle East today? Two significant events took place on March 27, 2002 on Passover Eve in the Israel. (the thirteenth day of the first month of the Jewish calendar)

The first event took place at a Passover Seder dinner at a hotel in Netanya, Israel. A suicide bomber walked into the hotel dining room and blew himself up massacring 28 innocent Israeli Jews celebrating Passover and wounded 168 innocent Israeli men, women and children.

This very night, Passover Eve, 2002, the Arab Summit in Lebanon officially came forth with the "Saudi Peace Plan". The "Saudi Peace Plan," like "the plan of Haman" was hatched on Passover Eve.

The Saudi Peace Plan *is* the Plan of Haman because it seeks to divide Israel, divide Jerusalem and create another Muslim nation on the land promised by God to Israel as an everlasting covenant.

This "Plan of Haman" will likely become the center piece of all the nations seeking to force Israel to return to the borders of pre-1967.

Many nations have embraced it. But "Haman's Plan" will *never* be "God's Plan for Israel!"

What is God's eternal plan for Israel? He revealed it in Genesis 17!

> *"I will establish My covenant between Me and you and your descendants after you throughout their generations for an <u>everlasting covenant</u>, to be God to you and to your descendants after you. I will give to you and to your descendants after you, the land of your sojournings, all the land of Canaan, for an <u>everlasting possession</u>; and I will be their God." Genesis 17:7-8*

In the days ahead we shall see if the "Plan of Haman", labeled today as the Saudi Peace Plan or the "Plan of God" prevails in Israel.

We read in the book of Esther that which made the difference as to whether Haman would succeed with his dastardly plan or not, was when Mordecai asked Queen Esther to go and stand before the king against the plan of Haman. At first Esther hesitated because it could cost her life if the King did not grant her an audience before him.

Esther was a beautiful, young Jewish woman. She had obtained favor with the king and he loved her. He chose Esther above all the young maidens of the land to be queen. But, as she was advised by her uncle, she did not make her heritage known and the king did not know that she was Jewish.

> *Then Mordecai told them to reply to Esther, "Do not imagine that you in the king's palace can escape any more than all the Jews. For if you remain silent at this time, relief and deliverance will arise for the Jews from another place and you and your father's house will perish. And who knows whether you have not attained royalty for such a time as this?" Esther 4:13-14*

Mordecai was calling Esther to *not* remain silent any longer, but to stand in the gap for her people.

Such a time as this has come once again where the Lord is looking for Mordecai's and Esther's who will not remain silent and will stand in the gap for Israel and the Jewish people. The question is, "Are *you* called for such a time as this to be an Esther or a Mordecai?"

If you have been called to be an Esther or Mordecai then understand that all the powers of the nations will be against you. You will be hated and cursed for taking a stand for Israel based on God's Word, rather than the wisdom of man. The powers and principalities of Satan along with the "Prophets of Jezebel" will come against you for standing with God's people.

Will you be like Esther when she declared?

> *Go, assemble all the Jews who are found in Susa, and fast for me; do not eat or drink for three days, night or day. I and my maidens also will fast in the same way. And thus I will go in to the king, which is not according to the law; and if I perish, I perish." Esther 4:16*

We ask you to pray the prayer of King Jehoshaphat as he stood before the Lord for his people.

> *"O LORD, the God of our fathers, are You not God in the heavens? And are You not ruler over all the kingdoms of the nations? Power and might are in Your hand so that no one can stand against You. Did You not, O our God, drive out the inhabitants of this land before Your people Israel and give it to the descendants of Abraham Your friend forever? They have lived in it, and have built You a sanctuary there for Your name, saying, Should evil come upon us, the sword, or judgment, or pestilence, or famine, we will stand before this house and before You (for Your name is in this house) and cry to You in our distress, and You will hear and deliver us.' Now behold, the sons of Ammon and Moab and Mount Seir, whom You did not let Israel invade when they came out of the land of Egypt (they turned aside from them and did not destroy them), see how they are rewarding us by coming to drive us out from Your possession which You have given us as an inheritance. O our God, will You not judge them? For we*

are powerless before this great multitude who are coming against us; nor do we know what to do, but our eyes are on You." II Chronicles 20:7-12

In this wonderful prayer, King Jehoshaphat revealed an understanding of where Israel was to turn to when the armies of the enemy were marching toward Jerusalem. He understood clearly that Israel's defense would come only from the God of Israel, rather than from their army. Only when the power of God went before the army of Israel would they prevail against their enemy. He knew no army could ever stand against God's army in battle.

The king's prayer was focused on God's heart, God's faithfulness and God's purpose for Israel. He gave recognition to the fact that it was God who gave Israel their inheritance, as the king referred to it in his prayer as *"Your possession" which "You gave us as an inheritance."*

By giving recognition to the fact that the enemies of Israel were marching toward Jerusalem for the specific purpose of removing Israel from their inheritance, the king was calling on the God of Israel to show His faithfulness to keep and defend His word to His chosen people.

The king's prayer revealed that it was not Israel's survival that was the real issue; rather it was God's faithfulness to His word, His promises and His inheritance. The enemy was seeking to prove that God's word and God's promises to Israel were worthless.

The king came before the Lord in humility, acknowledging who God is, and who he was. Again the king spoke the truth when he cried out to the Lord saying that Israel was helpless against this vast army coming against them. He knew only the Lord could defeat the enemies advancing toward them, and therefore the Lord would receive the glory, not man.

Notice that the king did not ask the God of Israel to destroy the army coming against them; rather he asked God the key question, "Will You not judge them?" King Jehoshaphat understood that God always judges those who come against His people, His word and His plan for Israel.

The king believed that where Israel, the land and the Jews are concerned, the God of Israel would never allow the plan of man to prevail over the word of God. His word, His promises and His plan for Israel will always prevail because the nations are nothing to Him. We are but mere men, and He is God.

GOD ANSWERS KING JEHOSHAPHAT'S PRAYER

"Listen, all Judah and the inhabitants of Jerusalem and King Jehoshaphat: thus says the LORD to you, 'Do not fear or be dismayed because of this great multitude, For the battle is not yours but God's. You need not fight in this battle; station yourselves, stand and see the salvation of the LORD on your behalf, O Judah and Jerusalem. Do not fear or be dismayed; tomorrow go out to face them, For the LORD is with you.'" II Chronicles 20:15, 17

In these verses we learn the absolute truth regarding God's eternal plan for Israel.

If all the nations of the earth join together and seek the destruction of Israel, they will not prevail. The nations may have all the oil, unlimited economic power, larger armies and greater military strength, outnumber Israel 100 to 1, but they will never prevail against God's eternal plan for the Nation of Israel because of God's answer to King Jehoshaphat in this eternal prayer

"The battle is not Israel's, but God's!"

The time is approaching once again when not only Israel but all believers will be called to "Stand and see the salvation of the Lord on behalf of Israel, Judah, and Jerusalem."

Where will you position yourself? Will you stand with the God of Israel and His people, or against them? If you position yourself *with* them you will have the Lord's promise just as it was given to Israel in the days of Jehoshaphat,

"DO NOT FEAR OR BE DISMAYED, FOR THE LORD IS WITH YOU!"

CHAPTER 28

THE CUP OF THE LORD OR THE CUP OF DEMONS

The Apostle Paul warned the church regarding turning away from Israel and being arrogant towards them, because he knew that is exactly what the church would do in the last days.

> *For I do not want you, brethren, to be uninformed of this mystery—so that you will not be wise in your own estimation—that a partial hardening has happened to Israel until the fullness of the Gentiles has come in; and so all Israel will be saved; just as it is written, "The Deliverer will come from Zion, He will remove ungodliness from Jacob." "This is My covenant with them, When I take away their sins." Romans 11:25-27*

Paul is speaking directly to the church, as he refers to them as "brethren" and warns them not to be wise in their own eyes. This warning is given with an explanation that the Lord has partially hardened the heart of Israel until the *"fullness of the Gentiles has come in."*

In Scripture, Israel is often referred to as the "fig tree." Jesus gave the church a specific word regarding the "fig tree" and what to do when you see it put forth its leaves.

> *"Now learn the parable from the fig tree: when its branch has already become tender and puts forth its leaves, you know that summer is near; So, you too, when you see all these things, recognize that He is near, right at the door." Matthew 24:32-33*

Israel is the *"fig tree"* and the Lord has raised it up to become a nation after 2,500 years of extinction. In 1948 it was a barren land with no trees of any kind. It was a wasteland and a swamp. Fifty-four years later, Israel is like a Garden of Eden, and its fruit has filled the nations of the earth.

The *"fig tree"* has put forth its branches, and the church is instructed by Jesus, "*When you see all these things, recognize that He is near, right at the door.*"

Recognize that Israel has put forth its branches, and the Lord is right at the door. This is important because the verses from Romans 11 tell us that when the "*time of the Gentiles*" draws to a close "*all Israel will be saved.*"

How will all Israel be saved and by whom? Paul gives us the answer in Romans 11.

> *"The Deliverer will come from Zion, He will remove ungodliness from Jacob." "This is My covenant with them, When I take away their sins." Romans 11:26-27*

The deliverer, the Messiah will come from Zion! Where is Zion? Zion is Jerusalem! He will *"remove the ungodliness from Jacob,* (Israel). *This is My covenant with them when I take away their sins."*

Only the Messiah, Jesus Christ can remove the sins of Israel. Only in the Bible is it prophesied that the Messiah will return to Jerusalem, and His feet will stand on the Mount of Olives.

> *Then the LORD will go forth and fight against those nations, as when He fights on a day of battle. In that day His feet will stand on the Mount of Olives, which is in front of Jerusalem on the east; and the Mount of Olives will be split in its middle from east to west by a very large valley, so that half of the mountain will move toward the north and the other half toward the south.*
> *Zechariah 14:3-4*

The Lord is coming again to Jerusalem, just as the prophecy declares. It will be a terrible day, a day of war when He goes forth and fights against the nations that have come against Israel, just as in the days of King Jehoshaphat.

Who are the nations that have come against Israel, and where will the Lord bring them to fight against Him?

Hasten and come, all you surrounding nations, And gather yourselves there. Bring down, O LORD, Your mighty ones. Let the nations be aroused and come up to the valley of Jehoshaphat, For there I will sit to judge All the surrounding nations. Put in the sickle, for the harvest is ripe. Come, tread, for the wine press is full; The vats overflow, for their wickedness is great. Multitudes, multitudes in the valley of decision! For the day of the LORD is near in the valley of decision. Joel 3:11-14

The Lord declares, *"Let the nations be aroused and come up to the valley of Jehoshaphat."* Where is this valley? This is the valley that runs between the Old City of Jerusalem and the Mount of Olives! Does this sound familiar? Is this not the *exact* area of contention in present day Jerusalem?

The Lord says He is going to bring the nations to this place, and there He will judge *"all the surrounding nations"* as well. Who are the "surrounding nations?" They are the Arab nations who have sought the destruction of Israel since her rebirth in 1948.

How great will this battle be? How much blood will flow from the wine press of God on the day He judges the nations?

And the angel swung his sickle to the earth, and gathered the clusters from the vine of the earth, and threw them into the great wine press of the wrath of God. And the wine press was trodden outside the city, and blood came out from the wine press, up to the horses' bridles, for a distance of two hundred miles. Revelation 14:19-20

On that day, from the great wine press of the wrath of God, blood will flow as high as horses' bridles for a distance of two hundred miles down through the Valley of Jehoshaphat! Can you even *imagine* that much blood?

When the Lord returns He will be returning as the Lord of Lords and the King of Kings, and He will enter into judgment with the nations and with the people of the nations that have sought Israel's destruction.

Nations are composed of people and, at that time, the Lord will also judge among the nations the people of the nations.

> *"But when the Son of Man comes in His glory, and all the angels with Him, then He will sit on His glorious throne. And all the nations will be gathered before Him; and He will separate them from one another, as the shepherd separates the sheep from the goats; and He will put the sheep on His right, and the goats on the left."*
> *Matthew 25:31-33*

The Lord and His angels are going to judge all the nations, and Jesus, as the great Shepherd of Israel, will separate them one from another. He will put the sheep on His right and the goats on His left.

> *"Then the King will say to those on His right, 'Come, you who are blessed of My Father, inherit the kingdom prepared for you from the foundation of the world. For I was hungry, and you gave Me something to eat; I was thirsty, and you gave Me drink; I was a stranger, and you invited Me in; naked, and you clothed Me; I was sick, and you visited Me; I was in prison, and you came to Me.'"*
> *Matthew 25:34-36*

Jesus is describing His sheep. They are easily distinguishable. Jesus is not speaking of Himself in these verses because He was never sick, naked or in prison. So, the sheep He is speaking about are *"His brethren."*

> *Truly I say to you, to the extent that you did it to one of these brothers of Mine, even the least of them, you did it to Me.*
> *Matthew 24:40*

The words used by Jesus here refer to, "(His) *brothers* (brethren) *of mine, even to 'the least of them,' you did it to Me."*

When you examine the words and search out the meaning of "brethren" or "brothers," you will find that it means, "belonging to the same people, or countryman."

Jesus was a Jew. His brothers were Jewish. His disciples were Jewish. The entire New Testament was written by Jews. These Jews all became believers in Jesus Christ as the risen Son of God.

Who then are "the least of them?" The meaning is "the smallest in size, or in the estimation of men."

Who is the smallest nation, with the fewest people in number, as well as the most hated and persecuted nation on earth? Who is deemed in the estimation of men to be the smallest, the least and the most persecuted? The Jews!

What race of people consistently throughout human history has often been naked, hungry, thirsty, often in prison, treated as strangers and considered outcasts among nations? The Jews!

This is a message that many in the church do not want to read or hear. However, these verses describe exactly who Jesus' "brethren" were, and who in His eyes was "the least of them."

Jesus is declaring, "What you did to my Jewish brethren, you did to Me!"

No President, Prime Minister, Pastor, Rabbi, King, Prince or individual can drink from the cup of the Lord and the cup of demons.

They are either *with* God and His people or *against* Him and His chosen people the Jews. There is no middle ground regarding His word, Israel, the Jews and Jerusalem.

Just as the Bible prophesied, the United Nations, the European Nations and the Arab nations have conspired with one mind against the God of Israel, the nation of Israel and His people so that Israel "will be a nation no more".

The "goats" are clearly distinguishable and described by Jesus, as they will all be put to His left. What will be their fate?

"Then He will also say to those on His left, 'Depart from Me, accursed ones, into the eternal fire which has been prepared for the devil and his angels.' And these will go away into eternal punishment, but the righteous into eternal life." Matthew 25:41, 46

When the Lord returns and judges the nations and the people, those who have cursed the Jews and Israel will be cast into eternal fire, but the righteous will enter into eternal life.

These verses contain the word of God regarding the judgment that will come to nations and people when He returns. The Jews are the plumb line, and He will hold nations and people accountable as to how they treated "His brethren."

Jesus' plan for Israel and the Jews is the same as it is for His church - redemption, salvation and eternal life. It has not changed from Genesis to Revelation, because God does not change nor can He lie.

The Apostle Paul, in Romans 11, said it beautifully, *"For the gifts and the calling of God are irrevocable."* Irrevocable, means irrevocable. What is the calling of God for Israel?

"Behold, days are coming," declares the LORD, "when I will make a new covenant with the house of Israel and with the house of Judah, not like the covenant which I made with their fathers in the day I took them by the hand to bring them out of the land of Egypt, My covenant which they broke, although I was a husband to them," declares the LORD. "But this is the covenant which I will make with the house of Israel after those days," declares the LORD, "I will put My law within them, and on their heart I will write it; and I will be their God, and they shall be My people. And they shall not teach again, each man his neighbor and each man his brother, saying, 'Know the LORD,' for they shall all know Me, from the least of them to the greatest of them," declares the LORD, "for I will forgive their iniquity, and their sin I will remember no more." Jeremiah 31:31-34

Just as Paul did in Romans 11, Jeremiah declares the Lord will enter into a new covenant with the house of Israel. Why? Because Israel is God's wife! Yes, His wife, as these verses declared, *"I was a husband to them!"*

This new covenant will be written on "hearts of flesh" rather than "tablets of stone." He will remove their sin and they shall all know Him, from the least of them to the greatest of them.

Then comes the last verse which is the most awesome verse ever written regarding the house of Israel.

Thus says the Lord, "For I will forgive their iniquity, and their sin I will remember no more."

When will the Lord make this new covenant with Israel?

> *"And it will come about in that day that I will set about to destroy all the nations that come against Jerusalem. And I will pour out on the house of David and on the inhabitants of Jerusalem, the Spirit of grace and of supplication, so that they will look on Me whom they have pierced; and they will mourn for Him, as one mourns for an only son, and they will weep bitterly over Him, like the bitter weeping over a first-born." Zechariah 12:9-10*

On the day that all the nations come against Jerusalem, the Lord God of Israel, the Messiah Jesus Christ will appear and destroy all the nations that have come against her.

On that incredible day, the Lord will *"pour out His Spirit on the house of David and on the inhabitants of Jerusalem."* What will be the result of His Spirit falling on the house of David and the inhabitants of Jerusalem?

The spirit of grace and supplication will open the eyes of all Israel and suddenly they will *"look upon Him whom they have pierced, and they will mourn for Him!"*

Why will they mourn for Him? Because when the spirit of grace and supplication is poured out upon the house of David, their hearts of stone will become hearts of flesh, and they will cry out, "My God and My Lord!"

In that one day, the entire remnant of the house of Israel will, "all know the Lord God of Israel, Jesus Christ from the least of them to the greatest!"

Will you choose to stand *with* God and His people and be counted among the sheep on His right, or will you choose to stand *against* them and be counted among the goats?

Your eternal destiny may well be determined by your decision!

> *"Behold, I am coming quickly, and My reward is with Me, to render to every man according to what he has done. I am the Alpha and the Omega, the first and the last, the beginning and the end." Revelation 22:12-13*
>
> *To those who are Jewish and to those who are Christians we say, "our theology may differ but what good is our theology if we do not love one another, when our Lord commanded us "to love one another as He loved us."*